TARGET IRAQ:

WHAT THE NEWS MEDIA DIDN'T TELL YOU

Jacket and interior design: Beau Friedlander
Typeface: Minion

Context Books
368 Broadway, Suite 314
New York, NY 10013
www.contextbooks.com

Library of Congress Cataloging-in-Publication Data

Solomon, Norman, 1951-
Erlich, Reese W. 1947-
  Target Iraq : what the news media didn't tell you / Norman Solomon and
Reese Erlich.
     p. cm.
  ISBN 1-893956-39-3
  1. United States--Military relations--Iraq--Press coverage. 2. Iraq--Military
relations--United States--Press coverage. 3. United States--Military policy--
Press coverage. 4. National security--United States--Press coverage. 5. Mass
media--Political aspects--United States. 6. Iraq--Politics and government--
1991---Press coverage. 7. Iraq--Social conditions--Press coverage. I. Title.
  E183.8.I72S67 2003
  070.4'49327730567'090511--dc21

                                                        2002156123

                        ISBN 1-893956-39-3

                           9 8 7 6 5 4

Manufactured in the United States of America

NORMAN SOLOMON
EXECUTIVE DIRECTOR, INSTITUTE FOR PUBLIC ACCURACY

REESE ERLICH
FOREIGN CORRESPONDENT

TARGET IRAQ:
WHAT THE NEWS MEDIA DIDN'T TELL YOU

INTRODUCTION BY **HOWARD ZINN**

AFTERWORD BY **SEAN PENN**

CONTEXT BOOKS
NEW YORK
2003

Table of Contents

Introduction by **HOWARD ZINN**

In all the solemn statements by self-important politicians and newspaper columnists about a coming war against Iraq, and even in the troubled comments by some who are opposed to the war, there is something missing. The talk is about strategy and tactics and geopolitics, and personalities. It is about air war and ground war, about alliances and weapons of mass destruction, and arms inspections, about oil and natural gas, about nation-building and "regime change."

What is missing is what an American war on Iraq will do to tens of thousands or hundreds of thousands of ordinary human beings who are not concerned with geopolitics and military strategy, and who just want their children to live, to grow up. They are not concerned with "national security" but with personal security, with food and shelter and medical care and peace.

I am speaking of those Iraqis and those Americans who will, with absolute certainty, die in such a war, or lose arms or legs, or be blinded. Or they will be stricken with some strange and agonizing sickness, which will lead to their bringing deformed children into the world (as happened to families in Vietnam, in Iraq, and also in the United States).

True, there has been some discussion of American casualties resulting from a land invasion of Iraq. But, as always when the strategists discuss this, the question is not about the wounded and dead as human beings, but about what number of American casualties would result in public withdrawal of support for the war, and what effect this would have on the upcoming elections for Congress and the presidency.

That was uppermost in the mind of Lyndon Johnson, as we have learned from the tapes of his White House conversations. He worried about Americans dying if he escalated the war in Vietnam, but what most concerned him was his political future. If we pull out of Vietnam, he asked his friend Senator Richard Russell, "they'll impeach me, won't they?"

In any case, American soldiers killed in war are always a matter of statistics. Individual human beings are missing in those numbers. It is left to the poets and novelists to take us by the shoulders and shake us and ask us to look and listen. In World War I, ten million men died on the battlefield, but we needed John Dos Passos to confront us with what that meant: In his novel *1919* he writes of the death of John Doe: "In the tarpaper morgue at Chalons-sur-Marne in the reek of chloride of lime and the dead, they picked out the pine box that held all that was left of . . . John Doe . . . the scraps of dried viscera and skin bundled in khaki. . . ."

Vietnam was a war that filled our heads with statistics, of which one stood out, embedded in the stark monument in Washington: 58,000 dead. But one would have to read the letters from soldiers just before they died to turn those statistics into human beings. And for all those not dead but mutilated in some way, the amputees and paraplegics, one would have to read Ron Kovic's account of how his spine was shattered and his life transformed, in his memoir *Born on the Fourth of July.*

As for the dead among "the enemy"—that is, those young men, conscripted or cajoled, or persuaded to pit their bodies against those of our young men—they are of no concern to our political leaders, our generals, our newspapers and magazines, our television networks. To this day, most Americans have no idea, or only the vaguest idea, of how many Vietnamese soldiers and civilians (actually, a million of each) died under American bombs and shells.

And for those who knew the figures, the men, women, children behind the statistics remained unknown until a picture appeared of a Vietnamese girl running down a road, her skin shredding from napalm, until Americans saw photos of women and children huddled in a trench as GIs poured automatic rifle fire into their bodies.

More than ten years ago, in the first war against Iraq, our leaders were proud of the fact that there were only a few hundred American casualties (one wonders if the families of those soldiers would endorse the word "only"). When a reporter asked General Colin Powell if he knew how many Iraqis died in that war he replied: "It's really not a number I'm terribly interested in." A high Pentagon official told the *Boston Globe:* "To tell you the truth, we're not really focusing on that question."

Americans knew that this nation's casualties were few in the Gulf War, and a combination of de facto government control of the press and the media's meek acceptance of that control ensured that the American people would not be confronted, as they had been in Vietnam, with Iraqi dead and dying.

There were occasional glimpses of the horrors inflicted on the people of Iraq—flashes of truth in the newspapers which quickly disappeared and then were lost. In mid-February, 1991, U.S. planes dropped bombs on an air raid shelter in Baghdad at four in the morning. Men, but mostly women and children, were huddled there to escape the incessant bombing. Four hundred to five hundred people were killed. An Associated Press reporter, one of few allowed to go to the site, said: "Most of the recovered bodies were charred and mutilated beyond recognition."

In the final stage of the Gulf War, American troops engaged in a ground assault on Iraq, which like the air war, encountered virtually no resistance. With victory certain and the Iraqi army in full flight, U.S. planes kept bombing the retreating soldiers who clogged the highway out of Kuwait City. A reporter called the scene "a blazing hell . . . a gruesome testament. . . .To the east and west across the sand lay the bodies of those fleeing."

That grisly scene appeared for a moment in the press and then disappeared in the exultation of a victorious war, in which politicians of both parties and the press joined. President Bush crowed: "The specter of Vietnam has been buried forever in the desert sands of the Arabian peninsula." The two major news magazines, *Time* and *Newsweek,* printed special editions hailing the victory in the war. Each devoted about a hundred pages to the celebration, mentioning proudly the small number of American casualties. They said not a word about the tens of thousands of Iraqis—soldiers and civilians—themselves victims first of Saddam Hussein's tyranny, and then of George Bush's war.

There were no figures on this—but more important, there was no photograph of a single dead Iraqi child, no names of particular Iraqis, no images of suffering and grief to convey to the American people what our overwhelming military machine was doing to other human beings.

This was brought home to me vividly in December, 1998, when the Clinton administration carried out a series of bombings on Iraq, again with no clue to the human consequences of those bombings. But an e-mail came to me from an Iraqi doctor:

"I am an Iraqi citizen who sought refuge here in the U.K. because of the brutality of Saddam's regime, which, within two years, killed my innocent old father and my youngest brother, who left a wife and children.... I am writing to you to let you know that during the second day of bombarding Iraq, a cruise missile hit my parents' house in a suburb of Baghdad. My mother, my sister-in-law (wife of my deceased brother),

and her three children were all killed instantly. . . . I am crying without tears. . . ."

The bombing of Afghanistan, once again, has been treated as if human beings are of little consequence. It has been
portrayed as a "war on terrorism," not a war on men, women,
children. The few press reports of "accidents" were quickly
followed with denials, excuses, justifications. There has
been some bandying about of numbers of Afghan civilian
deaths—but always numbers.

Only rarely has the human story, with names and images,
come through as more than a one-day flash of truth, as one
day when I read of a ten-year-old boy, named Noor
Mohammed, lying on a hospital bed on the Pakistani border,
his eyes gone, his hands blown off, a victim of American
bombs.

Surely, we must discuss the political issues. We note that
an attack on Iraq would be a flagrant violation of international law. We note that the mere possession of dangerous
weapons is not grounds for war—otherwise we would have to
make war on dozens of countries. We point out that the
country that possesses by far the most "weapons of mass
destruction" is our country, which has used them more often
and with more deadly results than any other nation on earth.
We can point to our national history of expansion and
aggression. We have powerful evidence of deception and
hypocrisy at the highest levels of our government.

But, as we contemplate an American attack on Iraq,
should we not go beyond the agendas of the politicians and
the experts? (John LeCarré has one of his characters say: "I

despise experts more than anyone on earth.") Should we not ask everyone to stop the high-blown talk for a moment and imagine what war will do to human beings whose faces will not be known to us, whose names will not appear except on some future war memorial?

Prologue

December 14, 2002: Near the center of Baghdad, along the Tigris River, an Iraqi woman showed a few foreigners around a water treatment plant that was seriously damaged during the Gulf War in early 1991. Our guide spoke in steady tones, describing various technical matters. But when someone asked about the possibility of war in 2003, her voice began to quaver.

A young American woman tried to offer comfort. She said, "You're strong."

"No," our guide responded emphatically. "Not strong." Tears welled in her eyes. Moments later she added, "We are tired."

She was speaking for herself, but also, it seemed, for most Iraqi people. After so much mourning, hardship and stress, they were exhausted—and frightened by what the future was likely to bring.

For an American in Baghdad, perhaps the most startling aspect of any visit was to encounter, up close and personal, Iraqis so routinely rendered invisible or fleeting by U.S. media coverage. It's all too easy to accept the bombing of people who have never quite seemed like people, whose suffering is abstract and distant. Looking them in the eyes can change that. In the words of my traveling companion on this trip, the actor and director Sean Penn: "I needed to come here and see a smile, see a street, smell the smells, talk to the people and take that home with me."

Driving through the streets of the impoverished Saddam City area of Baghdad, a UNICEF worker talked about the struggle to improve the health of children here; the gains have been hard-won and terribly slow. I could only imagine what another war would mean for them.

When we got to a primary school, the mood turned somber. Walls were crumbling. There was a smell of waste; the cement in the courtyard was sunken and the principal explained that rain sometimes caused it to fill with sewage. The teachers greeted us warmly; the students stared with large eyes, surprised and curious. Each small classroom held about sixty students. The windows didn't have glass; the benches were jammed with kids. Many of the children wore coats. Quite a few sat on the cold cement floor.

We visited another school, where the situation was similar. Then we went to a third school—one that had been reconstructed with UNICEF's help. The structures were solid; there was glass in the windows; the rooms were warm; the playground was nicely paved. The school felt well cared for, secure. Children were smiling, playing; there was laughter.

Hours later, Sean Penn and I were sitting in the office of Iraq's deputy prime minister, Tariq Aziz. Dressed in a business suit, he greeted us cordially. His voice reminded me of a foghorn. In a far corner, three large televisions were on, without sound, tuned to Iraqi TV, EuroNews and CNN International.

At the outset of the discussion, Penn said: "The politics for me are a side note to concern about my children, and the children of the United States, and the children of this country."

Aziz launched into a long explanation of why the United States should not attack Iraq. "Now we have brought the international inspectors, who are professionals, and they are doing their jobs freely, without any interruption. And still the warmongering language in Washington is keeping on." He continued: "Iraq is rich in its oil reserves. They want to take it away. But at what cost? At what cost for Americans, and for Iraq and for the whole region? Hundreds of thousands of people are going to die, including Americans— because if they want to take over oil in Iraq, they have to fight for it, not by missiles and by airplanes . . . they have to bring troops and fight the Iraqi people and the Iraqi army.

And that will be costly."

Asked about the White House's evident disappointment in the face of Iraqi cooperation with U.N. weapons inspectors, Aziz referred to the U.N. Security Council resolution adopted in early November. "They wrote this resolution, the last one, 1441, in a way to be certainly refused," Aziz said. "You know, sometimes you make an offer and you are planning to get a refusal. We surprised them by saying, 'OK, we can live with it. We'll be patient enough to live with it and prove to you and to the world that your allegations about weapons of mass destruction are not true.'"

Aziz's presentation was larded with propaganda. And given his longstanding loyal service to the mass-murderer Saddam Hussein, he could hardly be taken as any kind of moral authority. At the same time, many of the arguments that he used against a new war would be difficult to refute.

As the independent journalist I.F. Stone commented decades ago, "Every government is run by liars, and nothing they say should be believed." Stone was not equating all governments or asserting that they always lie. But he was pointing out that skepticism is essential, and no government's claims should be automatically accepted. It is our challenge and responsibility to sort through the propaganda of selective facts, distortions, and images in search of truth.

When a country goes on a war track, stepping out of line is always hazardous. All kinds of specious accusations fly. Whether you travel to Baghdad or hold an anti-war sign on Main Street back home, some people will accuse you of serving the propaganda interests of the foreign foe. But the only way to prevent your actions from being misconstrued is to do nothing. The only way to avoid the danger of having your words distorted is to keep your mouth shut.

In the functional category of "use it or lose it," the First Amendment remains just a partially realized promise. To the extent that it can be fulfilled, democracy becomes actual rather than theoretical. But that requires a multiplicity of voices. And when war demands our silence, the imperative of dissent becomes paramount.

We need to hear factual information and not let it be drowned out by the drumbeat of war. We need to think as clearly as possible. And we need to listen to our own hearts. When his visit to Iraq began, Sean Penn expressed the desire "to find my own voice on matters of conscience." In the near future, each of us will have that opportunity.

Norman Solomon
December 24, 2002

TARGET IRAQ:

WHAT THE NEWS MEDIA DIDN'T TELL YOU

Solomon: **Iraq at the Precipice**

September 13, 2002: At Saddam International Airport, an Iraqi official politely and firmly confiscated my satellite phone. This was no big surprise. I had just entered a totalitarian state, and Iraq's past encounters with incoming satellite-guided bombs were grim. After so many years of living under siege, any satellite-related technology was suspect, especially in the hands of an American. It would not be the last time that the Iraqi government came off this way: at once stupidly repressive and yet weirdly rational.

Less than an hour later, our delegation stood in front of the Al-Rashid Hotel. Television crews had staked out the front entrance. It was a little past two in the morning, and the lights from their cameras bathed the hotel's mosaic entryway with an eerie luminescence. At the curb, the congressman in the delegation hesitated, frowning as he looked at the entrance. Nick Rahall, a Democrat from West Virginia completing his thirteenth term in the U.S. House of Representatives, was a long way from home—the first member of Congress to set foot in Iraq during the presidency of George W. Bush.

Rahall eyed the TV cameras, and then looked once again at the marble mosaic. A sinister likeness of an earlier American president, George H. W. Bush, spanned the floor of the hotel entrance, along with tiles forming block letters that proclaimed "Bush Is Criminal." Carefully, the congressman edged sideways into the hotel lobby, screened by others to avoid the problematic photo-op.

With tensions steadily rising, the Iraqi propaganda seemed heavy-handed and easily dismissed. Throughout the capital city, countless pictures of Saddam Hussein were accompanied by preposterous odes of adulation. It was all rather crude. But as the United States and Iraq moved ever closer to war, many crucial realities were far too easy for Americans to ignore, or misunderstand, or evade.

Past the lobby in a back corner of the hotel's ground floor, next to the alcohol-free bar, guests could buy time on several computers in a little shop run by an earnest young man with a sparse but serviceable command of English and an evident desire to please. Day after day, he helped me and other foreigners to navigate his computer network and get onto the Web. His job description undoubtedly included monitoring customers for the government; yet his personal sincerity was unmistakable, and he had a sort of awkwardness that could not be faked. By the fourth day he was comfortable enough to tell me about the Protestant church where he went on Sundays, and to talk with me about his faith in Jesus "the Prince of Peace." On the same day, I got into a conversation with a British newspaper reporter who had stayed at the Al-Rashid in 1991 during the Gulf War, with frequent forays out to take a look at bomb damage caused by his government and mine. I was surprised to hear that even under those circumstances, the Iraqi people he met did not express hostility toward him; somehow, he said, the depth of their culture seemed to preclude hatred of the kind one might expect. I tried to imagine the shoe on the other foot: If Iraq's air force were bombing American cities, Iraqi visitors would surely be met with rage and hatred.

In the evening, our delegation went to an outdoor restaurant on the Tigris River. A cool breeze moved across the dark water; dozens of candle-lit tables stretched along the bank. It was a lovely evening, with couples and clusters of friends smiling and laughing as dusk became night under moonlight. Autumn had arrived. Soon this idyllic spot, on a river that had cradled civilization, was likely to become a war zone.

Tariq Aziz welcomed us into his office. The deputy prime minister was clearly a tough old guy in his military fatigues. A heavy aura of pessimism filled the room. Aziz presented his interpretation of the box that Washington had meticulously constructed for Iraq: "Doomed if you do, doomed if you don't."

The date was September 14, 2002. Sitting in Aziz's office were members of the delegation sponsored by the Institute for Public Accuracy—the congressman along with former U.S. Senator James Abourezk, Conscience International president James Jennings and myself. The Americans took turns contending that the ominous dynamic of recent weeks might be changed if—as a first step—Iraq agreed to allow unrestricted inspections. Yet it was hard to argue with Aziz when he said in formal English: "If the inspectors come back, there is no guarantee they will prevent war. They may well be used, in fact, as a pretext for provoking a new crisis." He was less than eager to grasp at weapons inspections as a way to stave off attack, suggesting instead that a comprehensive "formula" would be necessary for any long-term solution, presumably including a U.S. pledge of nonaggression and the lifting of economic sanctions.

Two days later, Iraq officially changed its position and announced a willingness to let U.N. weapons inspectors back into the country. Gauging the odds of averting war, the government in Baghdad chose a long shot—one that was at least better than no chance at all, but very risky nevertheless. Several years earlier, Washington had used Unscom inspectors for espionage purposes that were totally unrelated to the U.N.-authorized mission. In late 2002, new squads of inspectors poking around Iraq could furnish valuable data to the United States, heightening the effectiveness of a subsequent military attack.

"We are now a country facing the threat of war," the speaker of Iraq's National Assembly, Saadoun Hammadi, told us. "We have to prepare for that." A silver-haired man in frail physical condition, Hammadi was somber: "The U.S. administration is now speaking war. We are not going to turn the other cheek. We are going to fight. Not only our armed forces will fight. Our people will fight." As those words settled in the air, the gaunt old man paused, then added: "I personally will fight." At that moment, I thought I could see the dimming of light in his eyes, like embers in a dying fire.

The officials we met in Baghdad were clearly intelligent men, capable of reasonable discourse. Yet they served the regime of Saddam Hussein, subjecting Iraq's citizens to severe repression. Under his dictatorship, in the total absence of open debate, "civil society" could not really exist. Meanwhile, photos of Hussein in various poses—ceremonial, semiformal or warmly personal, sometimes enjoying a good chuckle—appeared daily on Iraq's front pages, presenting him as a fierce yet avuncular guardian of the people. His rule was simultaneously cartoonish and heinous, farce and tragedy.

A grotesque paradox was at work here. My country, a place of many democratic freedoms, was preparing to launch an unprovoked assault on a nation of people who found themselves trapped between a domestic tyrant and the U.S. government. The possibility of a peaceful solution appeared terribly remote; the magnitude of the suffering to come was difficult to comprehend.

The sky over Baghdad seemed to foreshadow new horrors, unfathomable yet still avoidable. Looking out at Iraq's capital city, I thought of something Albert Camus once wrote. "And henceforth, the only honorable course will be to stake everything on a formidable gamble: that words are more powerful than munitions."

From the twelfth floor of the Al-Rashid Hotel, the view was much like the spectacle of any large metropolis. Cars were in constant motion along the wide streets, and the cityscape was filled with tall buildings that receded into residential neighborhoods. There was nothing out of the ordinary here—except that if all went according to plan, my tax dollars would soon help to turn much of this city into hell.

As autumn began, a prominent *New York Times* article cited "senior administration officials" eager to sketch out a war plan: "Officials said that any attack would begin with a lengthy air campaign led by B-2 bombers armed with 2,000-pound satellite-guided bombs to knock out Iraqi command and control headquarters and air defenses." That kind of flat language makes for comfy reading.

The dynamics of distance, numbing to a far-off reality, and realpolitik made it easy for Washington to remain undisturbed during the previous dozen years of ruinous sanctions on Iraq. The effects of sanctions were on my mind when our delegation visited Baghdad's Al-Mansour Pediatric Hospital, where mothers sat on bare mattresses next to children who were languishing with leukemia and cancer. The youngsters were not getting adequate chemotherapy—a direct result of U.S.-led sanctions.

Walking through the cancer ward, I remembered a response from then-Secretary of State Madeleine Albright during a *60 Minutes* interview that aired on May 12, 1996. CBS correspondent Lesley Stahl stated "We have heard that a half a million children have died" and then asked: "Is the price worth it?" Albright replied, "I think this is a very hard choice, but the price—we think the price is worth it."

Consequences of the sanctions were ongoing. The U.S. Department of State continued to veto some crucial shipments of basic medical supplies to Iraq, including such items as special centrifuges for blood work, plasma freezers, and infusion pumps. After three visits to southern Iraq (most recently in September 2002), Dr. Eva-Maria Hobiger, an oncologist at Vienna's Lainz Hospital, said in heartfelt imperfect English: "By the support of these machines, the life of many sick children can be saved. It has to be called a crime when innocent and suffering children are the target of policy."

I would like to take all of Washington's politicians to visit a seven-year-old girl, suffering from leukemia, who we visited at the hospital. Perhaps they could have spared a few moments to look at the uncontrolled bleeding from her lips, the anguish in the fearful eyes of her mother.

In October 2002, a resolution sailed through the House and Senate to authorize a massive U.S. military attack against Iraq. I could almost hear the raspy and prophetic voice of Senator Wayne Morse roaring in 1964, the year he voted against the Gulf of Tonkin Resolution: "I don't know why we think, just because we're mighty, that we have the right to try to substitute might for right."

As with the years of sanctions and the deaths they caused, top officials in Washington—making a "very hard choice" for all-out war—still figured the human price would be "worth it." As geopolitical talk and strategic analysis dominated media coverage, the moral dimensions of war got short shrift.

I doubt many Americans would have felt at ease on a visit to the Al-Mansour Pediatric Hospital. I can only imagine, with horror, being in that hospital with missiles again exploding in Baghdad.

In late 2002, it was much easier to stick with comfortable newspeak about "a lengthy air campaign led by B-2 bombers armed with 2,000-pound satellite-guided bombs."

Erlich: **Media Coverage: A View from the Ground**

Reporters become real friendly, real fast in Iraq. You have a lot of shared experiences—from poor telecommunications to suspicious Iraqi officials to exasperating editors back home.

So Bert and I hit it off right away. Bert is the pseudonym I've chosen for a reporter with a major British media outlet. I'm not using his real name because I have no desire to get him in trouble. Reporters will tell things to each other they would never say publicly. So I'm inviting you into a metaphorical bar where, after a few beers, reporters let it all hang out. Bert and I had agreed to share a cab for a ride out of Baghdad. We passed over the city's modern freeways, reminders of the country's pre-sanctions wealth.

I mentioned that Saddam Hussein was rebuilding the ruling Baath party headquarters, which had been destroyed by a U.S. missile attack.

"He has lots of money for that," I noted casually.

"You'd get along fine with my editors," said Bert jovially, in an accent stuck partway between Oxford and south London. "They love to hear about Iraqi corruption and bad allocation of resources."

Bert is a political moderate highly critical of Hussein's government, but feels pressured by his much more conservative editors. "Whenever I propose stories showing the impact of sanctions on ordinary Iraqis," he said, "the editors call it 'old news.'" But the editors never tire of reworking old stories about corruption and repression in Iraq. Bert has internalized his editors' preferences and generally files stories he knows they will like. The alternative is to write stories that will either never get published or come out buried in the back pages.

The problem goes beyond disputes between reporters and editors. Most journalists who get plum foreign assignments already accept the assumptions of empire. I didn't meet a single foreign reporter in Iraq who disagreed with the notion that the U.S. and Britain have the right to overthrow the Iraqi government by force. They disagreed only about timing, whether the action should be unilateral, and whether a long-term occupation is practical.

Most people in the world, and much of the media outside the U.S. and Britain, still believe in national sovereignty, the old-fashioned notion enshrined in the U.N. Charter. No country has the right to overthrow a foreign government or occupy a nation, even if that nation horribly represses its own citizens. If the U.S. can overthrow Hussein, what prevents Russia from occupying Georgia or other former Soviet republics and installing friendlier regimes? The permutations are endless.

Despite numerous speeches and briefing papers, the Bush administration never convincingly demonstrated that Iraq poses an immediate threat to its neighbors. Unlike 1991 when Iraq occupied Kuwait, not a single nearby country has said it fears invasion from Iraq. The U.S. would never take a resolution to attack Iraq before the U.N. General Assembly because it would lose overwhelmingly. It prefers backroom deals in the Security Council.

When I raise the issue of sovereignty in casual conversation with my fellow scribes, they look as if I've arrived from Mars. Of course the U.S. has the right to overthrow Saddam Hussein, they argue, because he has weapons of mass destruction and might be a future threat to other countries. The implicit assumption is that the U.S.—as the world's sole superpower—has the right to make this decision. The U.S. must take responsibility to remove unfriendly dictatorships and install friendly ones. The only question is whether sanctions or invasion are the most effective means to this end.

The Bush and Blair administrations are fighting a two-front war: one against Iraq, another for public opinion at home. The major media are as much a battleground as the fortifications in Baghdad. And, for the most part, Bush and Blair have stalwart media soldiers manning the barricades at home.

The U.S. is supposed to have the best and freest media in

the world, but in my experience, having reported from dozens of countries, the higher up you go in the journalistic feeding chain, the less free the reporting.

The typical would-be foreign correspondent graduates from college and gets a job with a local newspaper or broadcast station. The pay is low and the hours long. (Small town newspaper reporters can still start out at less than $18,000 a year.) But after perhaps two years, they advance up the ladder to bigger media outlets. After five years or so, some of the more dedicated and talented reporters get jobs at big city dailies or in major market TV/radio stations. A few start out freelancing from abroad and then join a major media outlet, but they are in the minority.

That first few years of reporting are like boot camp. Even the best college journalism programs give you only the sketchiest ideas about real reporting. I know. I taught college journalism for ten years. The university never teaches you to find sources on fifteen-minutes notice, how to file a story from the field when cell phones don't work, or how to write an 800-word story in thirty minutes. The journalist's best education is on the job.

In addition to journalistic skills, young reporters also learn about acceptable parameters of reporting. There's little formal censorship in the U.S. media. But you learn who are acceptable or unacceptable sources. Most corporate officials and politicians are acceptable, the higher up the better. Prior to Enron's collapse, for example, CEO Ken Lay could be quoted as an expert on energy issues and the economy—despite what we know now to be his rather biased view of those topics.

Many other sources are deemed to be beyond the pale,

and are thus to be ignored or mocked. Black nationalists, progressive labor union advocates, or Marxists fall into this category. The same applies to conservatives outside mainstream Washington politics, such as conservative Muslims and certain rightwing intellectuals.

In Iraq I saw all this first hand. Let's look at Voices in the Wilderness, for example, a pacifist group based in Chicago. Some of their leaders had participated in a vigil in the Iraqi desert right up to the time America began bombing in the 1991 Gulf War. Voices in the Wilderness has brought hundreds of Americans to Iraq, including three congressmen in September 2002. It has community relief projects in Baghdad and has developed excellent contacts among nongovernmental organizations (NGOs).

One can agree or disagree with Voices in the Wilderness' views. I disagree with their pacifist approach, for example. But as journalists we should recognize them as a legitimate organization, part of a growing antiwar movement, which mobilized hundreds of thousands of people in Britain and the U.S. in September and October 2002.

But that's not the treatment they get from many major media. Ramzi Kysia, a Voices in the Wilderness organizer who lived in Baghdad, stopped by the press center one day to drop off a press release. He invited foreign reporters to cover a visit by American antiwar teachers to an Iraqi high school.

I was there when Kysia handed the press release to a TV crew. As soon as he left, the crew didn't even bother to read the entire press release before declaring that it was propaganda. They considered Voices to be outside the realm of legitimate sources, and therefore it could be safely ignored.

Indeed, a few weeks later when Voices held an antiwar march in Baghdad, John Burns of the *New York Times* reported the event in a mocking tone. He noted snidely that Saddam Hussein bans all demonstrations except those against America (*New York Times* 10/27/02). While Hussein certainly crushes dissenting opinion, the protests conducted by Americans in Baghdad who oppose U.S. policies are worthy of straight reporting. I cannot conceive of such a mocking tone permeating a *New York Times* story if Iraqi dissidents marched in Washington in support of U.S. policy.

The *Wall Street Journal* (11/4/02) treated Voices more straightforwardly but in the context of a humorous article about wacko westerners who visit Iraq as tourists.

In 1990 I took a group of my students to visit the *San Francisco Chronicle*. I have been contributing freelance stories to the *Chronicle* since 1989. I posed the following hypothetical story idea to then *Chronicle* Foreign Service editor David Hipschman. "What if I wanted to submit a story about Saddam Hussein's secret mistress?" I asked.

"I would want to see two sources backing up the claim," he said calmly. "And what if I had the same story saying President Bush [Sr.] had a mistress?" I asked. He laughed. "I'd want to see photos of the two of them in bed."

Every experienced reporter knows editors can set a standard of proof very low or impossibly high. If a reporter misquotes someone or gets some information wrong while writing an article critical of Saddam Hussein, editors back home are not likely to raise significant objections, but if an article critical of U.S. policy contains the same errors, all hell breaks loose. At a minimum, someone from the State Department or Pentagon calls to complain. Conservative media groups and radio talk show hosts may bring additional pressure. Raymond Bonner, a *New York Times* reporter who wrote accurate articles critical of U.S. policy in El Salvador, was reassigned from that country in the 1980s during just that sort of conservative campaign.

By the time reporters are ready to become foreign correspondents—a process that can take ten years or more—they understand how the game is played. Becoming a foreign correspondent is a plum job. It's interesting and challenging. You travel frequently and meet international leaders. You may see your byline on the front page. The job has gravitas.

And then there's the money. I've conducted an informal survey of foreign correspondent salaries in countries I've visited. (Remember, reporters say things to each other they wouldn't tell the public.) Salaries of full-time radio and print reporters at the major media that I've met range from $90–$125,000 per year. That doesn't count TV correspondents, who can make twice that much or more.

One *New York Times* reporter based in Africa told me over a beer one night that being a foreign correspondent is a great step in the career ladder at the *Times*. After a few years in Africa, he planned to move onto a more prestigious foreign assignment before working his way up the various editors' desks in New York. *Times* reporters are acutely aware of international trends, and if they are to win a Pulitzer Prize, they must report from a place of major importance. Right now Iraq and the Middle East fill the bill.

Money, prestige, career options, ideological predilections—combined with the down sides of filing stories unpopular with the government—all cast their influence on foreign correspondents. You don't win a Pulitzer for challenging the basic assumptions of empire.

Iraqi officials understood they wouldn't get fair coverage from many foreign correspondents. So what did they do? They responded with some of the most unsophisticated, ham-handed behavior I've ever experienced.

The process begins with getting an Iraqi journalism visa. A phone call to the Iraqi Interest Section at the end of 2002 revealed that the acquisition of a journalist visa might take two months or more. So I tried contacting various high level officials in Baghdad, who were friends of journalist friends. Strike out. The Iraqis are very suspicious of reporters they don't know, and even more suspicious of journalists whose stories they don't like.

Forget about sneaking into the country on a tourist visa as correspondents do in some repressive countries. (Hypothetical conversation with a border guard: I've always wanted to visit Babylon. And, by the way, are those anti-aircraft emplacements over there?)

Luckily, I learned about my coauthor's delegation to Iraq and got my name submitted on the list of reporters accompanying the congressman. We received our visas within ten days. Technically, the visas were only good for covering the delegation, but I correctly figured we could arrange to stay longer once in Baghdad.

All reporters had government guides, popularly called "minders." They helped set up interviews and served as interpreters. They also made sure you didn't go to certain places or interview certain people. To show the level of paranoia in Iraq, even NGOs such as Voices in the Wilderness had minders.

I developed a good rapport with my minder, and he was excellent at navigating the frustrating Iraqi bureaucracy to make interviews happen. I wasn't trying to visit a lot of controversial places. We were refused permission, however, to visit Saddam City, the most impoverished part of Baghdad.

In late October, after spontaneous demonstrations broke out demanding to know the whereabouts of Iraqi political prisoners, the government got very nervous about media coverage. It kicked out CNN's foreign correspondents and told other reporters they would be limited to ten-day journalist visas. Later in the year, the government allowed journalists to stay longer to cover the weapons inspectors' activities.

Such actions obviously intimidated reporters. They think: Will the content of my story result in expulsion from the country, or not being allowed to return? The Iraqi government uses various forms of intimidation, and it has led to self-censorship by some reporters.

It's a classic method used by those in power to intimidate reporters. If a U.S. president doesn't like certain coverage, the administration can make it impossible for the offending reporters to get insider interviews or it can refuse to return phone calls. Foreign reporters may be forced to leave the country. Reporters quickly learn to self-censor, or they're taken off the beat.

U.S. and Iraqi media policies have more in common than the leaders of either country would care to admit.

Solomon: The Media's War

For several decades, Helen Thomas covered the White House as a reporter for United Press International. She became a syndicated columnist at the start of the 21st century—and when the specter of war grew large in 2002, she didn't hold back. "It's bombs away for Iraq and on our civil liberties if Bush and his cronies get their way," Thomas said in early November during a speech at MIT. Looking back on a long career, she said: "I censored myself for fifty years when I was a reporter."

Although we may want journalists to keep their personal opinions out of news reporting, we might expect to be provided with all the relevant facts. This is rarely the case. A lot of key information gets filtered out. The process is often subtle in a society with democratic freedoms and little overt censorship. "Circus dogs jump when the trainer cracks his whip," George Orwell remarked more than half a century ago, "but the really well-trained dog is the one that turns his somersault when there is no whip." No whips are visible in America's modern newsrooms and broadcast studios. There are no leashes on editors, reporters, producers, or news correspondents. But in mainstream media, few journalists wander far.

"In truth, the strength of the control process rests in its apparent absence," media critic Herbert Schiller observed. "The desired systemic result is achieved ordinarily by a loose though effective institutional process." Schiller went on to cite "the education of journalists and other media professionals, built-in penalties and rewards for doing what is expected, norms presented as objective rules, and the occasional but telling direct intrusion from above. The main lever is the internalization of values." Conformity becomes habitual. Among the results is a dynamic that Orwell described as the conditioned reflex of "stopping short, as though by instinct, at the threshold of any dangerous thought . . . and of being bored or repelled by any train of thought which is capable of leading in a heretical direction."

In contrast to state censorship, which is usually easy to recognize, self-censorship among journalists is rarely out in the open. Journalists tend to avoid talking publicly about constraints that limit their work; they essentially engage in self-censorship about self-censorship. In the highly competitive media environment, you don't need to be a rocket scientist, or even a social scientist, to know that dissent does not boost careers. This is especially true during times of war. The rewards of going along to get along are clear; so are the hazards of failing to toe the line.

Occasional candor from big-name journalists can be illuminating. Eight months after 9/11, in an interview with BBC television, Dan Rather said that American journalists were intimidated in the wake of the attacks. Making what he called "an obscene comparison," the CBS news anchor ruminated: "There was a time in South Africa that people would put flaming tires around people's necks if they dissented. And in some ways the fear is that you will be 'necklaced' here, you will have a flaming tire of lack of patriotism put around your neck. Now it is that fear that keeps journalists from asking the toughest of the tough questions." Rather added that "I do not except myself from this criticism," and he went on: "What we are talking about here—whether one wants to recognize it or not, or call it by its proper name or not—is a form of self-censorship. I worry that patriotism run amok will trample the very values that the country seeks to defend."

On November 8, 2002, the same day that the U.N. Security Council approved its pivotal resolution about Iraq, National Public Radio's *All Things Considered* aired a story by longtime correspondent Tom Gjelten. "A war against Iraq would begin with a bombing campaign, and the resources for that phase of action are largely in place already," he reported. The tone was reassuring: "Defense officials are confident the U.N. timeline will not get in their way. For one thing, they're going ahead in the meantime with war preparations. Says one senior military officer, 'When the order does come, we have to be ready to rock 'n' roll.'"

"Ready to rock 'n' roll." It was a notable phrase for a high-ranking officer at the Pentagon to use with reference to activities that were sure to kill large numbers of people. The comment did not meet with any critical response; none of the news report's several hundred words offered a perspective contrary to the numbing language that distanced listeners from the human catastrophes of actual war. Such reporting is safe. Chances are slim that it will rankle government sources, news executives, network owners, advertisers or—in the case of "public broadcasting"—large underwriters. While NPR seems more and more to stand for "National Pentagon Radio," objections from listeners have apparently mattered little to those in charge. This should be no surprise. NPR's president and CEO, Kevin Klose, once served as director of the International Broadcasting Bureau, the U.S. government agency responsible for the Voice of America, Radio Free Europe, Radio Liberty, and Radio and Television Marti.

War planners and war makers have long relied on huge gaps between the horrendous realities of war and the professional news reporting about it. Even when the carnage was at its height in Vietnam, freelance correspondent Michael Herr later wrote, the U.S. media "never found a way to report meaningfully about death, which of course was really what it was all about. The most repulsive, transparent gropes for sanctity in the midst of the killing received serious treatment in the papers and on the air."

When war appears on the horizon, and especially after it begins, a heightened affliction seizes most American news outlets. The media spectacle becomes little more than the steady regurgitation of what's being fed from on high. The nation's media diet is stuffed with intensifying righteousness. Anchors, generals, Washington officials, reporters, and pundits fill television screens with analysis of tactics and strategies. The computer-simulated graphics push technical boundaries of dissimulation while the Pentagon tries out its latest war-fighting technologies.

Live satellite feeds have seemed to make war immediate, with viewers encouraged to ooh-and-ah while watching missiles strike Baghdad as though they were a fireworks display. The foremost mechanisms of numbing are commonly touted as the most enlightening. Television promises to bring war into our living rooms, but even as the blood flows and the agonies are endured far away, the coverage functions to make us more emotionally obtuse than ever. We're not only anesthetized; we may also be convinced that our awareness is being made more acute. With war, television accentuates myths of connectedness even as it further removes us from actual human connection.

"What do we see," media analyst Mark Crispin Miller has asked, "when we sit at home and watch a war? Do we experience an actual event? In fact, that 'experience' is fundamentally absurd. Most obviously, there is the incongruity of scale, the radical disjunction of locations. While a war is among the biggest things that can ever happen to a nation or people, devastating families, blasting away the roofs and walls, we see it compressed and miniaturized on a sturdy little piece of furniture, which stands and shines at the very center of our household. And TV contains warfare in subtler ways. While it may confront us with the facts of death, bereavement, mutilation, it immediately cancels out the memory of that suffering, replacing its own pictures of despair with a commercial—upbeat and inexhaustibly bright." All pretenses aside, the networks are factories of illusion: "The TV newsman comforts us as John Wayne comforted our grandparents, by seeming to have the whole affair in hand. . . . Since no one seems to live on television, no one seems to die there. And the medium's temporal facility deprives all terminal moments of their weight."

Major media outlets do provide some quality journalism. But the scattered islands of independent-minded reporting are lost in oceans of the stenographic reliance on official sources.

As any advertising executive knows, the essence of propaganda is repetition. Unless they're reverberating in the national media echo chamber, particular stories and perspectives usually have little effect.

In theory, everyone in the United States has freedom to speak his or her mind. Freedom to be heard is another matter. Sources of information and genuine diversity of viewpoints should reach the public on an ongoing basis, but they don't. Meanwhile, all kinds of pronouncements from official Washington take hold in news media while rarely undergoing direct challenge. The enormous distances between freedom of speech and freedom to be heard are partial explanations for why fervent belief in Uncle Sam's global benevolence remains so widespread among Americans. Laid on thick by the dominant voices of mass communication, the latest conventional wisdom flowing from the font of Pentagon Correctness swiftly hardens and calcifies. The mainstream news outlets are saturated with corporate sensibilities. The effects are such a matter of routine that we usually don't give them a second thought. While we might assume that coverage reflects the considered judgment of journalistic pros, those journalists are enmeshed in a media industry dominated by corporations with enough financial sway to redefine the meaning of functional professionalism.

We should never forget that war is big—very big—business.

William Hartung, a senior research fellow at the World Policy Institute based in Manhattan, pointed out in late 2002 that "the Bush administration's strategy of 'preemptive war' in Iraq is the brainchild of a small circle of conservative think tanks and weapons lobbying groups like the Project for a New American Century (PNAC), whose members have been pressing this approach for over a decade." Hartung added:

> In the run-up to the 2000 presidential election, PNAC published a report on "Rebuilding America's Defenses" which has served as a blueprint for the Bush/Rumsfeld Pentagon's military strategy, up to and including the coining of terms such as "regime change." PNAC's founding document—a unilateralist call for a return to the "peace through strength" policies of the early Reagan years—was signed by Paul Wolfowitz, Dick Cheney, Donald Rumsfeld, and numerous others who have

gone on to become major players in the Bush national security team. Like the Coalition for the Liberation of Iraq, a newly formed group of current and former Washington insiders designed to promote the Bush administration's policy in Iraq, PNAC draws its support from a tightly knit network of conservative ideologues, rightwing foundations, and major defense contractors. Bruce P. Jackson, a former vice president at Lockheed Martin who is a board member and a founding signatory of the Project for a New American Century's mission statement, serves as the chairman of the Coalition to Liberate Iraq. In adopting the strategy promoted by this conservative network, the Bush administration has successfully pressed for more than $150 billion in new military spending and arms export subsidies since September 11, 2001, much of which is going to major weapons makers like Boeing, Lockheed Martin, and Northrop Grumman.

Such vested interests in the military business are powerful forces in a media industry propelled by the corporate drive to maximize profits. The main problem with the U.S. media is profoundly structural. The airwaves supposedly belong to the public, but huge companies control them. Most of mass communication media—such as broadcasting, cable, newspapers, magazines, books, movies, the music industry, and, increasingly, the Web—are dominated by huge corporate entities. More and more, "public broadcasting" is also in the sway of big money. Along with the politically appointed board of the nonprofit Corporation for Public Broadcasting, corporate donors exert hefty influence on programs by "underwriting" specific shows.

And when war is on the agenda in Washington, news

coverage gets skewed to an extreme.

When the U.S. government improperly used U.N. weapons inspectors in Iraq for espionage purposes, the basic facts were widely but fleetingly reported by American media in early 1999—but during the months and years that followed, key facts about the spying and the serious damage it had done were not often reported. In 2002, media omissions and distortions about the matter were commonplace.

Much of the coverage was in sync with lies told repeatedly by senior U.S. officials such as Defense Secretary Donald Rumsfeld, who grew fond of claiming that Saddam Hussein had kicked out the U.N. weapons inspectors four years earlier. At a Pentagon news conference on September 3, 2002, with typical disregard for inconvenient facts, Rumsfeld said: "It is the Iraqis that ended the inspections; that we all know. We protested when the Iraqis threw the inspectors out. . . . Would it be nice if they had not thrown the inspectors out? Yes, that would have been preferable." Parroting of this particular lie has been bipartisan. In just one of many such instances, when Democratic senator John Kerry of Massachusetts appeared on MSNBC's *Hardball* in early autumn 2002, he categorically stated that Saddam Hussein "threw the inspectors out" in 1998.

Iraq did not expel the inspectors. Unscom head Richard Butler withdrew them in December 1998—just before a blitz of U.S. bombing dubbed "Operation Desert Fox."

With new inspections getting underway in late 2002, biological weapons scholar Susan Wright made a point that could not be grasped in the noncontext of evasive media coverage: "If the Iraqis detect that the U.N. inspection organization is being used for espionage once again, the inspections place Iraq in a double bind. If Iraq goes along, it would know that its defenses are being scrutinized. If it resists, its resistance may be used as a trigger for war by the United States government."

Even when American journalists mentioned the spying that had occurred the last time U.N. inspectors were in Iraq, it was usually downplayed or euphemized. Arguing for "legitimate cooperation between the inspectors and national intelligence agencies," Bill Keller of the *New York Times* wrote a November 16, 2002, op-ed piece that gingerly and swiftly glided past the historical record of U.S. spying: "The earlier Unscom inspection operation probably overstepped a line by helping the Americans eavesdrop, thus lending some credence to Saddam's anti-American rants."

More commonly in 2002, when referring to the espionage, news accounts transformed facts into mere allegations. (See Appendix One.) In the *New York Times* on August 3, Barbara Crossette reported that the Unscom team was disbanded "after Mr. Hussein accused the old commission of being an American spy operation and refused to deal with it." On the November 18 broadcast of NPR's *All Things Considered,* correspondent Vicky O'Hara said: "The last U.N. weapons inspection effort in Iraq fell apart amid accusations by Baghdad that inspectors were spying for the United States." The next day, the *Los Angeles Times* reported that four years earlier "Baghdad charged that there were spies on the team, and the United States complained that Iraq was using the accusation as an excuse to obstruct the inspectors."

A single short sentence in a *USA Today* news story by

John Diamond, which ran on August 8, 2002, was doubly deceptive: "Iraq expelled U.N. weapons inspectors four years ago and accused them of being spies." While the second part of the sentence is highly misleading, the first part is flat-out false. Several months later, *USA Today* was still refusing to print a retraction or correction.

Major news organizations kept repeating the lie as fact. A few examples:

> • *CBS Evening News,* November 9, 2002: "But as U.N. weapons inspectors prepare to return to Iraq for the first time since Saddam kicked them out in 1998, the U.S. faces a delicate balancing act: transforming the international consensus for disarmament into a consensus for war."

> • The *Washington Times,* November 14, 2002: "Iraq kicked out U.N. inspectors four years ago."

> • Bob Woodward in the *Washington Post,* November 17, 2002: "The speech assailed the United Nations for not enforcing the weapons inspections in Iraq, specifically for the four years since Hussein had kicked them out."

No product requires more adroit marketing than one that squanders vast quantities of resources while slaughtering large numbers of people.

America's euphemistic fog for war began several decades ago. It's very old news that the federal government no longer has a department or a budget named "war." Now, it's all called "defense," a word with a strong aura of inherent justification. The sly effectiveness of the labeling switch can be gauged by the fact that many opponents of reckless military spending nevertheless constantly refer to it as defense spending.

Since the 1980s, the intersection between two avenues, Pennsylvania and Madison, has given rise to media cross-promotion that increasingly sanitizes the mass destruction known as warfare. The first Bush administration enhanced the public relations techniques for U.S. military actions by "choosing operation names that were calculated to shape political perceptions," linguist Geoff Nunberg recalls. The invasion of Panama in December 1989 went forward under the name Operation Just Cause, an immediate media hit. "A number of news anchors picked up on the phrase Just Cause, which encouraged the Bush and Clinton administrations to keep using those tendentious names." As Nunberg points out, "it's all a matter of branding. And it's no accident that the new-style names like Just Cause were introduced at around the same time the cable news shows started to label their coverage of major stories with catchy names and logos." The Pentagon became adept at supplying video game-like pictures of U.S. missile strikes at the same time that it began to provide the wording of large-type captions for television screens.

Ever since the Gulf War in early 1991, people across the political spectrum have commonly referred to that paroxysm of deadly violence as Operation Desert Storm—or, more often, just Desert Storm. To the casual ear, it sounds kind of like an act of nature, or, perhaps, an act of God. Either way, according to the vague spirit evoked by the name Desert Storm, men like Dick Cheney, Norman Schwarzkopf and Colin Powell may well have been assisting in the implementation of divine natural occurrences: high winds and 2,000-pound laser-guided bombs raining down from the heavens. As the army's chief of public affairs, Major General Charles McClain, commented soon after the Gulf War ended: "The perception of an operation can be as important to success as the execution of that operation."

In October 2001, while launching missiles at Afghanistan, the Bush team came up with Operation Infinite Justice, only to swiftly scuttle the name after learning it was offensive to Muslims because of their belief that only Allah can provide infinite justice. The replacement, Enduring Freedom, was well received by U.S. mass media, an irony-free zone where only the untowardly impertinent might suggest that some people had no choice other than enduring the Pentagon's freedom to bomb.

Planning for U.S. military actions, White House operatives think like marketing executives. It was a candid slip of the tongue in the summer of 2002 when President Bush's chief of staff, Andrew Card, told the *New York Times:* "From a marketing point of view, you don't introduce new products in August." Not coincidentally, the main rollout of new-and-improved rationales for an upcoming war on Iraq did not take place until September.

The media spinners at the White House undoubtedly devoted considerable energy to sifting through options for how to brand the long expected U.S. assault on Iraq. And while most Americans would know its reassuring code name, we would never know the names of the Iraqi people killed in our names.

Erlich: **Voices from the Iraqi Streets**

Night has fallen on the dusty two-lane road in eastern Iraq when the taxi driver casually mentions that his family lives in a nearby town. When asked whether he would mind if an American visitor met his family, the taxi driver hits the brakes and swings the car around.

"Why not," he says with a smile.

After about a thirty-minute drive, the taxi skids to a halt on the dirt shoulder in front of a house in a working class district. The warren of small houses contains his extended family of twenty people: laborers, truck drivers, and a shopkeeper.

So begins one of the most forthright and honest interviews available to a reporter in Saddam Hussein's Iraq.

Reporters are normally accompanied at all times by a government "minder," whose mere presence can inhibit conversation. Even without the minder, Iraqis are cautious about political discussions if strangers are within earshot.

One brother is fluent in English. He speaks the most, and translates for the other family members.

"If there is war, we'll stay home," he said frankly. "We learned from the last war that going to shelters or the countryside doesn't help."

During the Persian Gulf War in 1991, the U.S. bombed the Ameriyah shelter in Baghdad, killing hundreds of people. The U.S. later claimed that the bunker was a command and control center for Hussein's military. Today, anyone can visit the site, which was turned into a museum, to see evidence that the people killed were civilians. Similarly, the U.S. bombed bridges in remote rural areas that resulted in civilian casualties.

It is not difficult to understand why many Iraqis have drawn the conclusion that it's wiser to sit at home than go to shelters or stay with relatives in the countryside.

While almost all Iraqis proclaim their support for Saddam Hussein in public, these family members, like many Iraqis, privately emphasized their dislike for the government. "Saddam has brought us nothing but war," said one family member, "but we also don't want the U.S. to invade our country."

Every Iraqi interviewed expressed a similar sentiment. Hatred of Saddam Hussein doesn't mean the people want America to occupy Iraq.

"We worry about the country splitting apart," said another family member. "It almost happened in 1991. Our friend here is Kurdish and he can't even go to see his relatives."

The friend, a man in his mid-thirties of Kurdish origin, explains that his family lives in the northern part of Iraq, now controlled by Kurdish groups under U.S. protection. He gave up visiting relatives because of hassles from both Iraqi and Kurdish authorities at the de facto border set up by the United States after the Gulf War.

The fear of a fractured nation is a valid concern. Many Iraqis worry that if the U.S. invades, the country will splinter into a Kurdish-controlled north and a Shia Muslim-controlled south. Even if there's not a formal division of the country, they say, the ethnic and religious differences threaten to fragment the country, as has happened in Afghanistan.

Bush's plan for a "regime change" is also a matter of grave concern. Iraqis worry about who will rule the new, post-Hussein Iraq. "We've never heard of most of these exiled leaders," says the brother, referring to the leaders of the Iraqi National Congress suggested by the U.S. as potential leaders of a post-Hussein government.

"And the king?" he continued, referring to the possibility that the U.S. would bring back a relative of King Faisal II, overthrown in 1958 as part of the country's fight against British colonialism. "Who remembers the king or knows anything about the monarchy now? Who will the U.S. anoint to rule the country—and how will this new leader do it?"

Some in the west are promoting the return of a monarch to Iraq much as the U.S. promoted Zahir Shah during the Afghanistan war. The eighty-eight-year-old king was widely hailed as a respected and popular alternative to the Taliban.

Only later was the American public to learn that Zahir Shah could barely speak and had no political base inside Afghanistan. Today he remains holed up in his Kabul palace without any significant role in the country.

The Bush administration understands that it won't be easy to replace Saddam Hussein. For all his dictatorial ruthlessness, Hussein managed to keep Iraq united. That's one reason why the U.S. and Britain supported the dictator during the 1980s.

As the U.S. invasion of Afghanistan shows, however, it's much easier to overthrow an old regime than to establish a functioning government, let alone a democratic one. Perhaps that's why the administration floated the possibility of installing a U.S. military general to run Iraq until local leaders can be vetted and installed. Understandably, the Iraqi people have a hard time understanding why a U.S. military dictator is better than a local one.

At the end of this impromptu group interview, the family patriarch says, "We are tired of war. We don't want another one with the U.S., or anyone else."

All of the Iraqis interviewed said they were tired of war, but some were willing to fight.

While most of Baghdad consists of concrete buildings built since the 1960s, the old center of Baghdad is still dotted with antique wood houses and shops. The Al Zahawi café looks like something out of a 1930s film. Men sit on wooden benches smoking water pipes filled with fragrant tobacco. Others slap dominoes on rough-hewn tables. There are only men here.

Ibrahim Jaleel, a forty-year-old clerk, has a different perspective on Iraq's recent wars. Jaleel says Iraqis are used to war—and will not be afraid if one comes again. Jaleel says he will resist if the U.S. invades.

"To the last drop of our blood we will fight and kill any foreigner who tries to occupy this land," he says. "According to Islamic teachings, we should defend three things: our country, our honor, and our property. To defend these things is martyrdom for us."

In saying this, Jaleel echoes the official government line, that Iraqis will fight door-to-door to repel a U.S. invasion. For some this is an expression of honest sentiment; many others will remain passive.

Downtown Baghdad is a noisy and gritty place. Drivers hit their car horns for any minor traffic problem; thin layers of dust cover most surfaces. Fadhil Hider's small store is a refuge from the cacophony. He sells pens, prayer beads and a seemingly infinite array of knickknacks.

At the age of sixty-one, Hider has lived through the era of British neocolonialism, when the monarchy ruled Iraq. In fact, he has a poster of King Faisal II clearly visible at the back of his shop. Asked if such open display of sympathy with the old regime ever caused him political problems, he shrugs and says "No." Asked if the royal family has any popular support in Iraq today, he shrugs and says "No" again.

Hider doesn't criticize Saddam Hussein, but he doesn't praise the leader either. Tellingly, Hider says nothing about resisting an American invasion. He expresses the helplessness felt by many Iraqis.

"What can we do? I'm going to shut down my shop. Many others will do so too. And we will wait for what will happen after that. It is a war between two states. One has highly sophisticated technology. The other does not." Hider expresses genuine outrage at the idea of a U.S. invasion, saying "foreign leaders shouldn't tell the Iraqi people what to do."

"If the Iraqi people want change, the change should be brought by the people themselves, not from outside. If there is some problem with the government, it should be changed by the people themselves—not by Blair or Bush or Chirac."

The University of Baghdad is a complex of dull, gray cement buildings, seemingly inspired by the architectural majesty of a Moscow apartment bloc. Students attend classes in rooms furnished with nothing but hard wooden chairs, and they have no air conditioning to combat the many days of blistering desert heat.

Lined up outside a professor's office waiting to get advice about classes, a number of students were eager to talk to an American reporter. Almost reflexively, some students recited what is expected of loyal Iraqis. Their proclamations would sound absurd by any standard.

"We like our President Saddam Hussein and are proud of him," says Reem Al Baikuty, a fourth-year English student. "We are proud of everything he does and everything he says." She then defends the omnipresent array of Saddam Hussein posters, paintings, murals and statues—a cult of personality that would have embarrassed Joseph Stalin.

Other students are less enthusiastic, however. While no one criticizes Hussein openly, some students indicate with shrugging shoulders and nods that Hussein has critics.

One graduate student, who asked that her name not be used, lived in the U.S. for ten years. She really liked Americans and the American system of government, she says, but then she returned to Iraq with her family and had to live through the Persian Gulf War.

"When we see the TV, we say the [American] people have everything. They've got great schools, great education, great lives. Why come and pick on people who are just starting in the world? I'm having a baby in April and I'm thinking 'Is this baby ever going to come? What situation will it be in?'"

This graduate student, who still has friends in America, says she and her husband face a terrible choice if U.S. troops enter Baghdad.

"My husband and I were talking about this the other day," she said. "If an American was to come to my door, he said 'I'd kill him.' I don't know what I would do."

Saad Hasani is the professor these students have come to see. He studied at Leeds University in Britain and teaches modern English drama at the University of Baghdad. In some ways, he's a man of two worlds—with one foot in western Europe and one in Iraq.

Professor Hasani quietly acknowledges that some western-oriented Iraqis might support a U.S. overthrow of President Hussein, but he says most Iraqis genuinely oppose it. He quotes an old Arabic saying: "Me and my brother against my cousin, but me and my brother and my cousin against a foreigner."

• • •

It's always hard for a reporter to know if people are expressing their true feelings. This reporter visited Afghanistan in January 2002 and interviewed dozens of people stopped at random. Virtually everyone said they hated the old Taliban regime and welcomed the American military. Even some people who had been injured or had family members killed by U.S. bombs expressed those sentiments.

If I had interviewed these very same people six months earlier, many would have praised the Taliban and denounced the U.S. Sometimes people say what they think you want to hear—and what's politically safe.

Americans shouldn't be too surprised by such attitudes. Imagine what you would do if a reporter showed up at your workplace and asked for a candid opinion of your boss and coworkers? Even if you were promised complete anonymity, you might still be a little circumspect. You might feel there was too much at stake. Were a new boss to come on board, you might feel more relaxed about criticizing the old boss, but you would remain cautious about commenting on the new one. Afghans and Iraqis are no different; they just have more to lose than their jobs.

After an invasion and occupation of Iraq, American reporters will certainly meet people critical of Saddam Hussein's regime. Some Iraqis will praise the American military. Are they telling the truth?

What would you say about your new boss?

Solomon: **Spinning 9/11, Terrorism, and Weapons of Mass Destruction**

> Those to whom evil is done
> Do evil in return.
>
> —W.H. Auden

In the early autumn of 2002, shortly before Congress voted to authorize a U.S. war against Iraq, a CBS News poll found that 51 percent of Americans believed that Saddam Hussein was involved in the attacks of September 11, 2001. Soon afterwards, the Pew Research Center reported that two-thirds of the U.S. public agreed "Saddam Hussein helped the terrorists in the September 11 attacks."

Around this time, a Washington correspondent for the Inter Press Service reported that "U.S. spy agencies appear unanimous that evidence linking Baghdad with the

September 11 attacks, or any attacks against Western targets since 1993, is simply non-existent." There was no factual basis for assertions of an Iraqi connection to those recent outbreaks of terrorism. But the surveys help to explain how the White House was able to gather support for targeting Iraq.

The Bush administration never hesitated to exploit the general public's anxieties that arose after the traumatic events of September 11, 2001. Testifying on Capitol Hill exactly fifty-three weeks later, Donald Rumsfeld did not miss a beat when a member of the Senate Armed Services Committee questioned the need for the United States to attack Iraq.

> Senator Mark Dayton: "What is it compelling us now to make a precipitous decision and take precipitous actions?"

> Defense Secretary Rumsfeld: "What's different? What's different is 3,000 people were killed."

As a practical matter, it was almost beside the point that allegations linking Baghdad with the September 11 attacks lacked credible evidence. A meeting allegedly took place in Prague between 9/11 hijacker Mohammed Atta and an Iraqi intelligence officer, but after many credulous reports in major U.S. media the claim was discredited (with the help of Czech president Vaclav Havel). Another flimsy gambit came when Rumsfeld charged that Qaeda agents had been given sanctuary by Saddam Hussein. As Britain's *Guardian* newspaper noted, "they had actually traveled to Iraqi Kurdistan, which is outside his control." Nevertheless, such deceptions often gain unflagging momentum. As Mark Twain once said, "A lie can go halfway around the world before the truth even gets its boots on."

Former CIA analyst Kenneth Pollack got enormous media exposure in late 2002 for his book *The Threatening Storm: The Case for Invading Iraq*. Pollack's book promotion tour often seemed more like a war promotion tour. During a typical appearance with CNN anchor Wolf Blitzer, who twice used the phrase "an important new book," Pollack explained why he had come to see a "massive invasion" of Iraq as both desirable and practical: "The real difference was the change from September 11th. The sense that after September 11th— the American people were now willing to make sacrifices to prevent threats from abroad from coming home to visit us here—made it possible to think about a big invasion force."

Middle East correspondent Robert Fisk was on the mark in the London *Independent* when, just after passage of the U.N. Security Council resolution in November 2002, he wrote, "Iraq had absolutely nothing to do with 11 September. If the United States invades Iraq, we should remember that." On many psychological levels, the Bush team was able to manipulate post-9/11 emotions well beyond the phantom of Iraqi involvement in that crime against humanity. The dramatic changes in political climate after 9/11 included a drastic upward spike in the attitude—fervently stoked by the likes of Rumsfeld, Dick Cheney and the president—that our military should be willing to attack potential enemies before they *might* attack us. Few politicians or pundits were willing to confront the reality that this was a formula for perpetual war, and for the creation of vast numbers of new foes who would see a reciprocal logic in embracing such a credo themselves.

President Bush's national security adviser "felt the administration had little choice with Hussein," reporter Bob Woodward recounted in mid-November 2002. A quote from Condoleezza Rice summed up the approach. "Take care of threats early."

Determining exactly what constitutes a threat—and how to "take care" of it—would be up to the eye of the beholder in the Oval Office.

Quite appropriately, the U.S. media response to 9/11 included horror, abhorrence and total condemnation. The terrorists' willingness to destroy and kill was evil. At the same time, the Pentagon's willingness to destroy and kill became more and more self-justifying in the closing months of 2002. As reporters and pundits echoed the assumptions of official Washington, the prospect of a new war on Iraq seemed more acceptable. There was scant concern for Iraqi civilians, whose last moments beneath incoming missiles would resemble those of the people who perished in the World Trade Center and Pentagon attacks.

"The greatest triumphs of propaganda have been accomplished, not by doing something, but by refraining from doing," Aldous Huxley observed long ago. "Great is truth, but still greater, from a practical point of view, is silence about truth." Despite the media din about 9/11, a silence—rigorously selective—has pervaded mainstream news coverage. For movers and shakers in Washington, the practical utility of that silence is immeasurable. In response to the mass murder committed by hijackers, the righteousness of U.S. military action remains clear—as long as implicit double standards remain unexamined.

On the morning of September 11, 2001, while rescue crews braved the intense smoke and noxious rubble, ABC News analyst Vincent Cannistraro helped to put the unfolding events in perspective for millions of TV viewers. Cannistraro is a former high-ranking official of the Central Intelligence Agency. He was in charge of the CIA's work with the contras in Nicaragua during the early 1980s. After moving to the National Security Council in 1984, he became a supervisor of covert aid to Afghan guerrillas. In other words, Cannistraro has a long history of assisting terrorists—first, contra soldiers who routinely killed Nicaraguan civilians; and then mujahedeen rebels in Afghanistan such as Osama bin Laden.

How could a longtime associate of state-sponsored terrorists now be on record denouncing terrorism? It's easy. All that's required is for media coverage to engage in business as usual by remaining in a non-historical zone that has no use for inconvenient facts. In his book *1984*, George Orwell described the mental dynamics: "The process has to be conscious, or it would not be carried out with sufficient precision, but it also has to be unconscious, or it would bring with it a feeling of falsity and hence of guilt. . . . To tell deliberate lies while genuinely believing in them, to forget any fact that has become inconvenient, and then, when it becomes necessary again, to draw it back from oblivion for just so long as it is needed, to deny the existence of objective reality and all the while to take account of the reality which one denies—all this is indispensably necessary."

Secretary of State Colin Powell denounced "people who feel that with the destruction of buildings, with the murder of people, they can somehow achieve a political purpose." Powell was describing the hijackers who had struck his country hours earlier. Unintentionally, he was also describing a long line of top officials in Washington. Surely U.S. policymakers had believed that they could "achieve a political purpose" with "the destruction of buildings, with the murder of people" when they opted to launch missiles at Baghdad in 1991 or Belgrade in 1999. But U.S. media scrutiny of killings perpetrated by the U.S. government is rare. Only some cruelties merit the spotlight. Only some victims deserve empathy. Only certain crimes against humanity are worth our tears.

"Spin" is often achieved with a single word. In the world of public relations, success or failure can depend on the public's responses to particular buzzwords. Ever since the attacks of 9/11, no buzzword has seen more usage than "terrorism." During the first two days of October 2001, CNN's website displayed an odd little announcement. "There have been false reports that CNN has not used the word 'terrorist' to refer to those who attacked the World Trade Center and Pentagon," the notice said. "In fact, CNN has consistently and repeatedly referred to the attackers and hijackers as terrorists, and it will continue to do so."

The CNN disclaimer was accurate, and by conventional media standards reassuring. But it bypassed a basic question: Exactly what goes under the heading of terrorism?

For this country's mainstream journalists, that's a non-question about a no-brainer. More than ever, the proper function of the terrorist label seems obvious. "A group of people commandeered airliners and used them as guided missiles against thousands of people," said NBC News executive Bill Wheatley. "If that doesn't fit the definition of terrorism, what does?"

True enough. At the same time, it's notable that American news outlets routinely label groups as terrorist using the same criteria as the U.S. government. Editors generally assume that reporters don't need any formal directive—the appropriate usage is simply understood. In sharp contrast, the global Reuters news agency has stuck to a distinctive approach for decades. "As part of a policy to avoid the use of emotive words," the news service says, "we do not use terms like 'terrorist' and 'freedom fighter' unless they are in a direct quote or are otherwise attributable to a third party. We do not characterize the subjects of news stories but instead report their actions, identity and background so that readers can make their own decisions based on the facts."

Reuters reports from 160 countries. The terrorist label is highly contentious in quite a few of them. Behind the scenes, many governments have tried to pressure Reuters into "spinning" coverage by using the terrorist label to describe their enemies. From the vantage point of government leaders in

Ankara or Jerusalem or Moscow, the news media should label their violent foes "terrorists." From the vantage point of embattled Kurds or Palestinians or Chechens, the news media should label the violent leaders in Ankara or Jerusalem or Moscow "terrorists," too.

In October 1998, scholar and activist Eqbal Ahmed made some recommendations to America. The first one: "Avoid extremes of double standards. . . . Don't condone Israeli terror, Pakistani terror, Nicaraguan terror, El Salvadoran terror, on the one hand, and then complain about Afghan terror or Palestinian terror. It doesn't work. Try to be even-handed. A superpower cannot promote terror in one place and reasonably expect to discourage terrorism in another place. It won't work in this shrunken world."

If American reporters expanded their working definition of terrorism to include all violence committed against civilians to pursue political goals, they would meet with fierce opposition in high places. During the 1980s, with a nonevasive standard for terrorism, news accounts would have labeled the Nicaraguan contra guerrillas—in addition to the Salvadoran and Guatemalan governments—perpetrators of U.S.-backed terrorism.

In the political lexicon of America, terrorism—as used to describe, for example, the killing of Israelis—cannot also be used to describe the killing of Palestinians. Yet, in an October 2002 report, the Israeli human rights group B'Tselem documented that 80 percent of the Palestinians killed recently by the Israeli Defense Force during curfew enforcement were children. Twelve people under the age of sixteen had been killed, with dozens more wounded by Israeli gunfire in occupied areas, during a period of four months. "None of those killed endangered the lives of soldiers," B'Tselem said.

Professor of politics George Monbiot helped to provide context for the White House's moral stance toward Iraq, in an August 2002 column for the *Guardian,* when he assessed "the prospect of George Bush waging war on another nation because that nation has defied international law." Monbiot pointed out: "Since Bush came to office, the United States government has torn up more international treaties and disregarded more U.N. conventions than the rest of the world has in twenty years. It has scuppered the biological weapons convention while experimenting, illegally, with biological weapons of its own. It has refused to grant chemical weapons inspectors full access to its laboratories, and has destroyed attempts to launch chemical inspections in Iraq. It has ripped up the antiballistic missile treaty, and appears to be ready to violate the nuclear test ban treaty. It has permitted CIA hit squads to recommence covert operations of the kind that included, in the past, the assassination of foreign heads of state. It has sabotaged the small arms treaty, undermined the international criminal court, refused to sign the climate change protocol and, last month, sought to immobilize the U.N. convention against torture."

No double standard has been employed more flagrantly in the Middle East than the U.S. policy regarding "weapons of mass destruction." In the world according to Washington and major American news media, U.S. policymakers have always enjoyed the unquestionably high moral ground in confrontations with Iraq's dictator.

A portion of the British daily press has been appreciably more skeptical. "Respected scientists on both sides of the Atlantic warned yesterday that the U.S. is developing a new generation of weapons that undermine and possibly violate international treaties on biological and chemical warfare," *Guardian* correspondent Julian Borger reported from Washington on October 29, 2002. The scientists "also point to the paradox of the U.S. developing such weapons at a time when it is proposing military action against Iraq on the grounds that Saddam Hussein is breaking international treaties. Malcolm Dando, professor of international security at the University of Bradford, and Mark Wheelis, a lecturer in microbiology at the University of California, say that the U.S. is encouraging a breakdown in arms control by its research into biological cluster bombs, anthrax and non-lethal weapons for use against hostile crowds, and by the secrecy under which these programs are being conducted." Professor Dando warned that the United States "runs the very real danger of leading the world down a pathway that will greatly reduce the security of all."

"The security of all" has been a central rationale for war against Iraq—with the specter of nuclear weapons in the hands of Saddam Hussein serving as a crowning argument. In August of 2002, Vice President Cheney was so eager to play the nuclear scare card that he said Iraq would acquire nuclear arms "fairly soon," contradicting CIA reports that Iraq could not do so for at least five more years.

During a mid-summer 2002 interview for the book *War On Iraq* by William Rivers Pitt, former U.N. weapons inspector Scott Ritter discussed Iraq's nuclear weapons program: "When I left Iraq in 1998, when the U.N. inspection program ended, the infrastructure and facilities had been 100 percent eliminated. There's no debate about that. All of their instruments and facilities had been destroyed. The weapons design facility had been destroyed. The production equipment had been hunted down and destroyed. . . . We can say unequivocally that the industrial infrastructure needed by Iraq to produce nuclear weapons had been eliminated."

When chief U.N. inspector Hans Blix arrived in Baghdad on November 18, 2002, his comments included expressing hope for "a zone free of weapons of mass destruction in the Middle East as a whole." That's not a concept that gets much news coverage in the United States, and this instance was no exception; a search of all the major U.S. daily papers in the Nexis database found Blix's statement quoted only by the *Washington Post* (and paraphrased by the *Atlanta Journal-Constitution*). Yet, as the *Scotsman* newspaper reported the same day, Blix was referring to "the Security Council's original measures in the wake of the Gulf War of 1991, which in theory outlined a nuclear-free zone to cover Iraq's neighbors Iran and particularly Israel."

Richard Butler—one of Blix's predecessors as the U.N. chief weapons inspector—had amassed a record of congeniality toward the U.S. government, but after returning home to Australia he made some critical statements about the superpower's approach to nuclear weapons: "My attempts to have Americans enter into discussions about double standards have been an abject failure even with highly educated and engaged people," Butler said. The disconnect had to do with the nuclear arsenals of the United States and its allies—including Israel. When he delivered the Templeton Lecture at the University of Sydney in the early fall of 2002, Butler recalled: "Amongst my toughest moments in Baghdad were when the Iraqis demanded that I explain why they should be hounded for their weapons of mass destruction when, just down the road, Israel was not, even though it was known to possess some 200 nuclear weapons."

Much public knowledge of Israel's nuclear weaponry can be traced to the courageous efforts of a former Israeli nuclear technician named Mordechai Vanunu. At the time of Butler's university lecture, whistle blower Vanunu was completing his sixteenth year behind bars in Israel. (Many of the years passed in solitary confinement.) Vanunu has been a nonperson in U.S. news media, for reasons having everything to do with the kind of "double standards" that Butler cited.

On September 30, 1986, Israel's government kidnapped Vanunu in Rome and put him on a cargo ship. Back in Israel, at a secret trial, he faced charges of espionage and treason. A military court sentenced him to eighteen years in prison. Vanunu had provided journalists at the *Sunday Times of London* detailed information about Israel's arsenal of nuclear bombs.

After growing up in a Jewish family, Mordechai Vanunu became an employee at the Dimona nuclear plant in 1976. Nearly a decade later, shortly before his employment ended at the remote nuclear facility, he took photos inside Dimona, which has always been closed to international inspection.

Using severance pay to travel abroad in 1986, Vanunu contacted the famous Insight investigative unit of the *Sunday Times*. "During his extensive debriefing by our Insight team," the newspaper reported, "he offered to give the paper his photographs and all his information for nothing provided we did not publish his name, insisting his sole interest was in stopping nuclear proliferation in the Middle East."

The *Sunday Times* persuaded Vanunu to allow his name to be used. The paper agreed to pay Vanunu for serialization or a book based on his information, but money did not seem to motivate him. "My impression of the man was of someone who had a genuine desire to tell the world of something that was going on which he felt was genuinely wrong for Israel to do," said Peter Hounam, the main reporter on the story for the *Sunday Times*. "He felt it was wrong that the Israeli public and parliament were not given any information about what was happening in Dimona."

On October 5, 1986, the *Sunday Times* broke the story under the front-page headline "Revealed: The Secrets of Israel's Nuclear Arsenal." By then Vanunu was already a prisoner of the Israeli government.

If you mention Mordechai Vanunu's name to an American, you're likely to get a blank look. On the western side of the Atlantic, he's a media phantom. But imagine what would have happened if another country in the Middle East—say, Iraq—kidnapped one of its citizens to punish him for spilling the beans about its nuclear weapons program. That person would have become an instant media hero in the United States.

Erlich: **Depleted Uranium: America's Dirty Secret**

During the Persian Gulf War, the U.S. military wreaked havoc on Iraqi tanks and armored vehicles. The Iraqis didn't stand a chance because the U.S. tanks were protected with metal called depleted uranium. Depleted uranium (DU) armor and ammunition gave the U.S. a decided advantage. U.S. tanks fired DU shells, and helicopter Gattling guns sprayed .30 mm DU ammunition in a deadly rain that may well be killing U.S. veterans and Iraqi civilians years after the war ended.

Depleted uranium is the material left over from the processing of nuclear fuel. The U.S. military uses DU as a substitute for lead to fill the core of special ammunition. Depleted uranium is 1.7 times denser than lead, so it slices through enemy armor and fortifications with relative ease when compared to its lead counterpart. The same material is layered into tank armor to prevent penetration by enemy shells.

When DU ammunition hits a hard target, the impact causes intense heat, and the pulverized DU enters the air. Soldiers nearby breath it in. Winds can blow it miles away from the area of initial impact, so unlucky civilians also inhale it. DU remains radioactive for 4.5 billion years. It can contaminate soil and seep into the water table. Critics worry that DU is creating long-term environmental disaster areas in both Iraq and former Yugoslavia, where the U.S. also used DU. Doctors in both areas report huge increases in cancer rates, and Iraqis have seen a big jump in birth defects as well. Gulf War veterans report some of the same symptoms.

Any U.S. and Britain invasion of Iraq will almost certainly see the extensive use of depleted uranium ammunition once again. In addition to the many civilian deaths caused by direct hits, the ammunition may well cause great suffering and death long after the conflict.

Basra, Iraq

Something is very, very wrong in southern Iraq. At Basra's Children's and Maternity Hospital, doctors display a large photo album of hundreds of children born with horrible birth defects. One study conducted by Iraqi doctors indicated that 0.776 percent of Basra-area children were born with birth defects in 1998, compared to just 0.304 percent in 1990, before the Gulf War. Another study showed a rise in childhood cancers and other malignancies of 384.2 percent from 1990–2000.

According to Dr. Jinan Hassan, a pediatrician and assistant professor at the Basra University Medical College, "Iraqi women from the south are afraid to get pregnant because they are afraid of malformation. . . . At the time of birth, mothers used to ask if their child was a boy or girl. Now they ask 'Is it normal or abnormal?'"

Iraqi doctors, and an increasing number of western scientists, attribute the rise in diseases and birth defects to the U.S. and British use of depleted uranium. Iraqi doctors said they have found highly elevated rates of cancers in those parts of Basra where depleted uranium ammunition was used. The Pentagon confirms firing 320 tons of DU ammunition during the Gulf War.

U.S. and British army veterans also suspect DU as a cause of Gulf War illnesses. Dr. Doug Rokke, now a major in the U.S. Army Reserves, was in charge of cleaning up twenty-four U.S. tanks hit by American DU shells during the Gulf War, casualties of friendly fire. He and his crew worked for three months shipping the armor back to the U.S. for special decontamination.

The exposure to DU contamination was so intense, Rokke told me, "We all got sick within seventy-two hours." Three years later, Rokke said, a urine test showed that he had 5,000 times the permissible level of uranium in his body. A number of Gulf War veterans who worked in DU-contaminated zones have been diagnosed with the same kind of cancers as found in Basra civilians, and they also fathered children with birth defects.

Rokke, a physicist with a Ph.D. and the U.S. Army's former DU Project Director, studied the military's internal documents and prepared materials on how to clean up DU contaminated areas. Based on his experience, he says, "The United States military leaders knew that using DU would cause health and environmental problems."

The Pentagon argues, however, that DU ammunition poses no danger to civilians. Department of Defense literature notes that depleted uranium is less radioactive than uranium found naturally in the environment, and argues that even uranium miners regularly exposed to large doses of natural uranium suffer no ill health as a result.

The Department of Defense concedes that small amounts of depleted uranium are absorbed into the body when breathed or eaten. But "no radiological health effects are expected because the radioactivity of uranium and depleted uranium are so low." (*www.gulflink.osd.mil*)

Health trends in Iraq and former Yugoslavia indicate the Pentagon may be horribly wrong. Austrian oncologist Dr. Eva-Maria Hobiger has studied the link between depleted uranium, cancer, and birth defects. She won't draw any conclusions unless an extensive epidemiological study can be done in Basra. The Iraqi studies of birth defects and cancer rates have not been verified by outside scientists.

Hobiger notes, however, that if DU lodges in sensitive parts of the body such as lymph nodes or bones, it produces a low but steady stream of radiation. Over time, this could cause cancer, she says.

Dr. Hobiger and many others note that southern Iraq has been an environmental disaster area for years. During the Iran-Iraq War, some residents were hit with poison gas. After the Persian Gulf War, Iraqi troops set oil wells on fire and polluted the entire region for months. There is also an air pollution problem—largely from industrial plants and brick factories—in southern Iraq. Some scientists contend that these other environmental factors could be causing the health problems in Basra.

Dr. Hobiger argues that these other environmental factors, while dangerous, don't explain all the problems. Air pollution, for example, isn't known to cause birth defects. While some poison gases can cause birth defects among parents who breathe the gas, they are not known to cause malformations long after initial exposure.

She theorizes that DU in combination with the air pollution may cause the cancer problems. DU's chemical toxicity may also play a role. As a heavy metal, the DU can get into the ground water and soil. Once in the food chain, it can cause kidney cancer and a host of other ailments.

Until recently, however, scientists didn't know whether DU actually appeared in the bodies of people living in Iraq and the Balkans. That's because scientists must conduct a very sophisticated urine analysis of each patient to find the DU, and those tests were not available in Iraq.

The Pentagon and various other NATO armies did conduct such tests on their soldiers who fought in the Balkan wars and reported they found no traces of DU.

Then in 2001, BBC-TV in Scotland commissioned Professor Nick Priest to study the issue. He's a professor at the School of Health, Biological and Environmental Sciences at London's Middlesex University and a recognized expert in radiation issues. He took urine samples from twelve people from Bosnia and Kosovo who lived in areas hit with DU ammunition.

Some were cancer patients, and one was a child born after the Bosnian war. All showed some traces of DU in their systems. The test "most likely indicates that the metal [DU] is now present in the food chain and/or drinking water," Professor Priest wrote in a report for a scientific journal. In an interview in London, Priest said that the older the people were, the more DU they had in their systems, indicating that the contamination comes from DU particles in the environment that are slowly absorbed over time.

In October 2002, Professor Priest and scientists from Germany conducted a study with a larger number of Serbs and Bosnians to determine whether his original findings can be replicated. The results were expected to be released in 2003.

Professor Priest doesn't think that the amount of radiation emitted from depleted uranium poses a serious health hazard for civilians. The amount of DU he found, even in the cancer patients, was below what could be expected to cause such health problems. He noted that DU contains less radiation than natural uranium.

The controversy continues because no one can explain the sharp increase in Iraqi birth defects and cancers since the Gulf War. It's extremely difficult to link an individual's disease to a specific environmental factor. Scientists need to conduct a study to correlate the types of health problems and where they occur geographically. With a large enough sample, they could determine if the health problem was caused by exposure to DU, other environmental factors, family history, or something else.

At one time the World Health Organization was planning just such a study in Iraq, but couldn't find the funding. It was blocked by the U.S. and British, according to Dr. Hobiger.

Doctors are also troubled by reports of health problems in Bosnia similar to those found in Basra. U.S. planes fired approximately 3.3 tons of DU shells during the 1994–1995 Bosnian war and 10.2 tons during the 1999 Kosovo war, according to the U.S. Department of Defense.

In interviews with doctors from Serbia and Bosnia who have examined patients living in areas where DU ammunition was extensively fired, they've seen a sharp increase in cancer cases, although so far, there has been no increase in birth defects.

Dr. Nada Cicmil-Saric is a medical oncologist who treated families from the town of Foca-Srbinje, Bosnia. The town's bridge was destroyed by U.S. attacks in 1994. She found numerous cases where two or more family members living near the bridge suffered from malignancies. While some cases might be attributed to genetic factors, in other cases husbands and wives both developed malignancies after 1994, a highly unusual occurrence, according to Dr. Cicmil-Saric.

At her hospital, which treats many people exposed to DU, she reports a five-fold increase in lung cancer and three-fold increase in lymph node cancers since 1994—both of which could be triggered by DU exposure. She has also seen a five-to six-fold increase in breast cancer, which is generally not associated with DU, indicating other factors may be at work.

In the Bosnian war, as well as the 1998 NATO bombing of Serbia during the Kosovo war, the U.S. hit factories and power stations, causing the release of carcinogenic smoke. As a result—much like the situation in Iraq—doctors say it's hard to isolate the impact of DU without a thorough epidemiological study.

Officials in the Yugoslav republics of Montenegro and Serbia aren't waiting for a final scientific assessment of DU dangers. They have already started to clean up DU contaminated sites.

Cape Arza is a spectacularly beautiful spot about 30 miles south of Dubrovnik, in Montenegro along the Adriatic coast. According to local myth, God was carrying treasure from the Middle East to Europe and dropped some of it on this land. In summertime, locals swim and fish in the azure sea.

On May 29 and 30, 1999—the closing days of the Kosovo war—two U.S. A-10 Thunderbolt (Warthog) planes fired DU rounds into Cape Arza. The Yugoslav Army built bunkers there in 1968, which had been used during the war with Croatia in the early 1990s. But there were no troops or weapons there in 1999, according to Tomislav Andelic, a physicist with the Center for Toxicological Research of Montenegro. "The U.S. just made a mistake," Andelic said, "they had bad intelligence."

The U.S. planes shot some 300 DU .30 mm bullets into Cape Arza, scattering them over 20,000 square meters of deserted land.

Over the past three years, the DU bullets have begun to oxidize and crumble. Montenegrin authorities worry that the DU dust could be blown by the wind or seep into the ground. Campers pitching a tent or children playing with the bullets could become contaminated. In addition, the existence of contaminated land will ruin any chance of tourism along this scenic stretch of seacoast.

The Yugoslav Army sealed off the area. The Montenegrin government kicked in $300,000 and the federal Yugoslav government another $100,000 to clean up Cape Arza. Soldiers holding gamma monitors on long wooden dowels painstakingly covered every inch of ground looking for DU bullets. They carefully pulled them out by hand like archeologists working an ancient dig. The contaminated bullets and radioactive dirt were shipped to Belgrade for storage with other low-level radioactive waste.

The federal Yugoslav government plans to clean up five similar sites in Serbia. But neither Serbia nor Montenegro can find a foreign government, international agency, or NGO willing to contribute money for the cleanups.

"If any country recognizes the need of cleaning up depleted uranium," said Andelic, "it would automatically mean they recognized the danger coming from DU. If this happened, we could have damage claims and nobody is ready to accept this."

If even some of the claims by Iraqi and Balkan doctors about DU prove correct, then the U.S. and Britain would come under tremendous pressure to stop using DU ammunition and could potentially be forced to pay billions of dollars in compensation to victims.

Somehow, this doesn't fit into U.S. plans to remain the world's only superpower.

In closing, it is worth noting that both the U.S. and British armies have taken extensive precautions when test firing DU shells in their own countries. Soldiers are enshrouded in protective suits and use respirators when firing tank shells. The test areas are sealed off and soldiers isolate the destroyed armor and tank rounds after the tests.

Solomon: **Unilateral by Any Other Name**

When the U.N. Security Council adopted its Iraq resolution on November 8, 2002, American politicians and journalists hailed the unanimous vote as a huge victory for international cooperation, and a breakthrough that averted unilateral action. In Washington, a range of lawmakers sounded upbeat. So did pundits eager to congratulate the Bush team for a diplomatic job well done.

New York Times eminence Thomas Friedman was close to ecstatic. "For a brief, shining moment last Friday," his November 13 column declared, "the world didn't seem like such a crazy place." To Friedman and countless other promoters of Washington's latest conventional wisdom, the United

Nations had proven its worth by proving its value to the White House. "In the world of a single, dominant superpower, the U.N. Security Council becomes even more important, not less," Friedman wrote. Among the benefits: "The Bush team discovered that the best way to legitimize its overwhelming might—in a war of choice—was not by simply imposing it, but by channeling it through the U.N."

If the United Nations serves as a conduit for American power, we are still in the realm of unilateralism. Massive geopolitical, economic, and military strength enables the United States to gain Security Council votes, international acquiescence, and even some combat allies. It's an old story: Decades ago, the U.S. government claimed that the Vietnam War was an "allied" effort because it included participation from Filipino, Australian, and South Korean troops.

Pulled into the agenda-building of U.S. war planners, the U.N.'s Security Council provided tremendously important fig leaves. In Friedman's words, "The American public told Karl Rove, and the British public told Tony Blair, that Iraq was a war of choice, and while it may be a legitimate choice, they did not want to fight it without the cover of the U.N. and the support of its key member states."

To get the Good War-Making Seal of Approval from the United Nations, the Bush administration handed out major plums while flexing Uncle Sam's muscles. "Backroom deals with France and Russia regarding oil contracts in a postwar Iraq were a big part of the picture," U.N. analyst Phyllis Bennis wrote in *The Nation* after the Security Council vote. "And the impoverished nation of Mauritius emerged as the latest poster child for U.S. pressure at the U.N. The ambassador, Jagdish Koonjul, was recalled by his government for failing to support the original U.S. draft resolution on Iraq. Why? Because Mauritius receives significant U.S. aid, and the African Growth and Opportunity Act requires that a recipient of U.S. assistance 'does not engage in activities that undermine U.S. national security or foreign policy interests.'"

The Mauritius episode tracked with broader patterns. The Security Council vote "was a demonstration of Washington's ability to wield its vast political and economic power," Inter Press Service reported. Nations on the council "voted under heavy diplomatic and economic pressure from the United States." Most of the countries were recipients of aid from Washington and "were seemingly aware of the fact that in 1990 [during the lead-up to the Gulf War] the United States almost overnight cut about $70 million in aid to Yemen immediately following its negative vote against a U.S.-sponsored Security Council resolution to militarily oust Iraq from Kuwait."

In the British magazine the *New Statesman,* author John Pilger recalled some sordid details of the pre-Gulf War object lesson in superpower payback. "Minutes after Yemen voted against the resolution to attack Iraq, a senior American diplomat told the Yemeni ambassador: 'That was the most expensive No vote you ever cast.' Within three days, a U.S. aid program of $70 million to one of the world's poorest countries was stopped. Yemen suddenly had problems with the World Bank and the IMF, and 800,000 Yemeni workers were expelled from Saudi Arabia. . . . When the United States sought another resolution to blockade Iraq, two new members of the Security Council were duly coerced. Ecuador was warned by the U.S. ambassador in Quito about the 'devastating economic consequences' of a No vote. Zimbabwe was threatened with new IMF conditions for its debt."

During the autumn of 2002, compounding the impacts of Washington's prodigious carrots and sticks, a parallel reality of American dominance loomed large; the United States pointedly reserved the right to do whatever it wanted anyway. In this context, while the compromises that went into Resolution 1441 made it less blatantly a red-white-and-blue instrument, the U.S. concessions were likely to be of little long-term significance. In any event, the approved resolution's text was riddled with contradictions and deceptions. "Many paragraphs of this new resolution are simply dripping with double standards," said Denis Halliday, a former U.N. Assistant Secretary General who had headed the United Nations oil-for-food program in Iraq. "Much in this resolution should apply to all states in the region violating Security Council resolutions and possessing weapons of mass destruction." (See Appendix Three.)

Forty-eight hours after the Security Council resolution passed 15-0, White House Chief of Staff Andrew Card said on NBC: "The U.N. can meet and discuss, but we don't need their permission" before launching a military attack. "The U.S. and our allies are prepared to act," Card explained, and he summed up the bottom line: "If we have to go to war, we will." Meanwhile, on CNN, the Secretary of State had the same message: "If he [Saddam Hussein] doesn't comply this time, we'll ask the U.N. to give authorization for all necessary means, and if the U.N. is not willing to do that, the United States, with like-minded nations, will go and disarm him forcefully."

Nine days later, speaking to some members of Parliament in Britain, the Pentagon's Defense Policy Board chair Richard Perle dispensed with the pretense that war would hinge on what happened with U.N. weapons inspectors. "George Bush's top security adviser last night admitted the U.S. would attack Iraq even if U.N. inspectors fail to find weapons," the *Mirror* reported on November 20. "Perle stunned MPs by insisting a 'clean bill of health' from U.N. chief weapons inspector Hans Blix would not halt America's war machine. Evidence from ONE witness on Saddam Hussein's weapons program will be enough to trigger a fresh military onslaught, he [Perle] told an all-party meeting on global security."

The Perle argument was that U.N. inspection teams could not prove a negative. "All he [Blix] can know is the results of his own investigations. And that does not prove Saddam does not have weapons of mass destruction." Perle's threshold for launching an all-out war was notably low: "Suppose we are able to find someone who has been involved in the develop-ment of weapons and he says there are stores of nerve agents. But you cannot find them because they are so well hidden. Do you actually have to take possession of the nerve agents to convince?"

A former British defense minister, Peter Kilfoyle, responded with candor: "Because Saddam is so hated in Iraq, it would be easy to find someone to say they witnessed

weapons building. Perle says the Americans would be satis-
fied with such claims even if no real evidence was [*sic*] produced. That's a terrifying prospect." Kilfoyle said that
"America is duping the world into believing it supports these
inspections. President Bush intends to go to war even if
inspectors find nothing. This makes a mockery of the whole
process and exposes America's real determination to bomb
Iraq."

In mid-November, U.N. officials involved in the inspection process made public statements to the effect that a minor
Iraqi offense should not be viewed as a "material breach" of
the resolution. Secretary General Kofi Annan said that a
"flimsy" excuse should not be sufficient for going to war. But
such utterances did nothing to mitigate an overarching reality: In sharp contrast to the U.N. Charter's provision that "all
Members shall refrain in their international relations from
the threat or use of force against the territorial integrity or
political independence of any state," the United States government would be the ultimate arbiter of compliance or breach.
At the Center for Constitutional Rights in New York, the
organization's president Michael Ratner was blunt: "What is
going on here is completely outrageous. The Security
Council, a body that was supposed to make war at the behest
of one country illegal and impossible, is paving the way to a
war of aggression. And worst of all, the U.S. will be able to
argue that somehow it has its blessing."

There was substantial irony, even breathtaking hypocrisy, in
the proclamations by top U.S. officials that they would make
war on Iraq—with or without the backing of a U.N. Security

Council resolution—if in their judgment Iraq had failed to obey a U.N. Security Council resolution. But such contradictions are standard ingredients in the newspeak that pervades U.S. views of the United Nations.

News coverage of the United Nations gets confusing sometimes. Is the U.N. a vital institution or a dysfunctional relic? Are its Security Council resolutions profoundly important for international relations, or beside the point because global leadership must now come from the world's only superpower?

Americans kept hearing that the United States would need to mount a full-scale attack on Iraq because Saddam Hussein had violated U.N. Security Council resolutions, at the same time that we were told the U.S. government must reserve the right to take military action if the Security Council failed to make appropriate decisions about Iraq.

To clarify the situation, here are three basic guidelines for understanding how to think in sync with America's leading politicians and pundits:

• U.N. resolutions approved by the Security Council are very important, and worthy of enforcement with massive military force, if the White House says so. Otherwise, the resolutions have little or no significance, and they certainly can't be allowed to interfere with the flow of American economic, military, and diplomatic support to any of Washington's allies.

Several countries have continued to ignore large numbers of resolutions approved by the U.N. Security Council since the early 1990s. Morocco remains in violation of more than a dozen such resolutions—as does Israel—and Turkey is also violating quite a few. Top officials in those nations aren't expecting ultimatums from Washington anytime soon.

• Some U.N. resolutions are sacred. Others are superfluous. To cut through the media blather about Security Council resolutions that have been approved in past years, just keep this in mind: In the world according to American news media, the president of the United States possesses Midas-like powers over those U.N. resolutions. When he confers his regal touch upon one, it turns into a golden rule that must be enforced. When he chooses not to bless other U.N. resolutions, they have no value.

• The United Nations can be extremely "relevant" or "irrelevant," depending on the circumstances.
When the U.N. serves as a useful instrument of U.S. foreign policy, it is a vital world body taking responsibility for the future and reaffirming its transcendent institutional vision. When the U.N. balks at serving as a useful instrument of U.S. foreign policy, its irrelevance is so obvious that it risks collapsing into the dustbin of history.

Pretty words function as window-dressing for war-making. "There's a lot of lofty rhetoric here in Washington about the U.N.," said Erik Leaver, a researcher with the Foreign Policy in Focus project. Stephen Zunes, an associate professor of politics at the University of San Francisco, cited some key facts in mid-November 2002: "There are more than 100 U.N. Security

Council resolutions being violated by member states. Iraq is in violation of at most sixteen of them. Ironically, Washington has effectively blocked the enforcement of U.N. Security Council resolutions against many other nations, since they include such countries as Morocco, Indonesia, Israel and Turkey that are allied with the United States."

Leaver was thinking outside the media box when he asked this vital question: "If the U.S. takes military action using the cover of the United Nations, what is to prevent other countries from launching their own military attacks in the name of enforcement of U.N. resolutions—against Turkey in Cyprus, or Morocco in Western Sahara, or Israel in Palestine? This is precisely the reason why the doctrine of preemptive force is a dangerous policy for the United States to pursue."

Some key information about U.N. weapons inspectors in Iraq briefly surfaced on the front pages of American newspapers in early January of 1999 before promptly vanishing. Nearly four years later, with righteous war drums beating loudly in Washington, retrieving the story meant reaching deep down into the news media's Orwellian memory hole. "U.S. Spied on Iraq Under U.N. Cover, Officials Now Say," a front-page *New York Times* headline announced on January 7, 1999. The article was unequivocal: "United States officials said today that American spies had worked undercover on teams of United Nations arms inspectors ferreting out secret Iraqi weapons programs. . . . By being part of the team, the Americans gained a first-hand knowledge of the investigation and a protected presence inside Baghdad." A day later, a follow-up *Times* story pointed out: "Reports that the United States used the United Nations weapons inspectors in Iraq as cover for spying on Saddam Hussein are dimming any chances that the inspection system will survive."

With its credibility badly damaged, the U.N. inspection system did not survive. Another factor in its demise was the U.S. government's declaration that the severe sanctions against Iraq would remain in place whether or not Baghdad fully complied with the inspection regimen. Few American news accounts illuminated such facts or allowed them to interfere with the conditioned media reflex of blaming everything on Saddam Hussein.

During the last half of 2002, instead of presenting a full summary of relevant past events, mainstream U.S. journalists and politicians were glad to routinely focus on tactical pros and cons of various aggressive military scenarios. While some pundits raised warning flags, even the most absurd Swiss-cheese rationales for violent "regime change" in Baghdad frequently passed without mainstream challenge.

In late July, the *Wall Street Journal* published an essay by a pair of ex-Justice Department attorneys who claimed that the U.S. would be "fully within its rights" to attack Iraq and overthrow the regime based on "the customary international law doctrine of anticipatory self-defense." The nascent contradiction here: If "anticipatory self-defense" amounted to a valid reason for starting a war, the Iraqi government could use the same excuse to justify an attack on the United States (even if we set aside the fact that U.S. bombing of the unilaterally declared "no fly zones" in Iraq had been going on for years).

During the late summer and fall of 2002, there was something pathetic—and dangerous—about the crush of liberal commentators pinning their hopes on Colin Powell. The secretary of state was a hallowed "moderate" (compared to the likes of Dick Cheney and Donald Rumsfeld), and news outlets breathlessly chronicled the twists and turns of his intragovernmental struggles. He won accolades for being a patient and shrewd Washington insider who was also a consummate diplomat. In the march to war and the search for common ground, he was a superb drum major and a mainstream media darling.

Some bastions of rightwing media clout, such as the *Wall Street Journal* editorial page, condemned him as insufficiently militaristic. But in the real world—rather than undermining prospects for a military conflagration in Iraq—Powell's outsized prestige was a very useful asset to war planners. The retired general "is seen by many of Washington's friends and allies abroad as essential to the credibility of Bush's foreign policy," the French news agency AFP noted in early September. He had the wisdom to patiently line up a myriad of diplomatic ducks before the big shooting commenced. By midautumn, *Newsweek*'s "Conventional Wisdom" feature had Powell's arrow pointing skyward: "Brilliant diplomacy wins over France, Syria AND hawks."

Even pundits who recognized the grisly underbelly of his deadly role offered adulation. "We should be glad that Colin Powell is secretary of state," Mary McGrory wrote six weeks before the end of 2002. "Were it not for him, our soldiers might even now be going door to door in downtown Baghdad conducting a lethal canvass." Yet, as the prominent *Washington Post* columnist pointed out, Powell "didn't tell the president not to go to war; he told him how to go to war in a politically correct way." Instead of trying to prevent a war, Powell "only tried to put it off for a couple of weeks and provide a fig leaf."

The media legend of Colin Powell celebrates his high jumps over low standards. Powell's record does not belong to a man of conscience. Avid participation in the deplorable has been integral to his career. A few examples:

• Serving as a top deputy to Secretary of Defense Caspar Weinberger, Powell supervised the army's transfer of 4,508 TOW missiles to the CIA in January 1986. Nearly half of those missiles became part of the Reagan administration's arms-for-hostages swap with Iran. Powell helped to hide that transaction from Congress and the public.

• As President Reagan's national security adviser, Powell became a key operator in U.S. efforts to overthrow the elected government of Nicaragua. When he traveled to Central America in January 1988, Powell threatened a cutoff of U.S. aid to any country in the region that refused to go along with continued warfare by the contra guerrillas, who were then engaged in killing thousands of Nicaraguan civilians. Powell worked to prevent the success of a peace process initiated by Costa Rica's president, Oscar Arias.

• When U.S. troops invaded Panama on December 20, 1989, Powell was chairman of the Joint Chiefs of Staff. He had "emerged as the crucial figure in the decision to invade," according to British newspaper reporter Martin Walker. Hundreds of civilians died in the first hours of the invasion. Powell declared on that day: "We have to put a shingle outside our door saying, 'Superpower lives here.'"

• In late 2000, while Bush operatives were going all-out during the Florida recount to grab the electoral votes of a state where many thousands of legally qualified African Americans had been prevented from voting due to Republican efforts, Powell went to George W. Bush's ranch in Texas to pose for a photo-op and show support for his presidential quest.

But the Gulf War in 1991, more than any other event, catapulted Powell to the top ranks of American political stardom. The main media controversy dogging Powell about the war has been the question of whether the U.S.-led forces should have marched on Baghdad to overthrow Saddam Hussein. Other, deeper questions have gone unexamined.

On September 25, 1995, during the San Francisco leg of a nationwide book tour for Colin Powell's best-selling autobiography, dozens of reporters and photographers packed into a room baking under the hot lights of television cameras. There was a wave of excitement when Powell arrived and strode to the rostrum. He was the picture of confident authority, with his wire-rim executive-style glasses, well-tailored pinstripe black business suit, crisp pastel-blue shirt, and tasteful burgundy tie. The mayor pumped Powell's hand and proclaimed a formal welcome for the first African American to serve as chairman of the Joint Chiefs of Staff.

Reporters competed to toss some softball questions, which the retired general smoothly swatted over the fence. One query was about race; another inquired about the upcoming '96 presidential campaign; then Powell began to explain why Americans again were dazzled by the military a quarter century after the disreputable Vietnam War. While Powell was enumerating recent military successes—"the superb performance of the armed forces of the United States in recent conflicts, beginning with the, I think, Panama invasion, and then through Desert Shield and Storm"—a voice broke in from the back of the room. A middle-aged man in a wheelchair was speaking. Hunched in his metal contraption, his jeans-clad legs dangling inert, he shouted, "You didn't tell the truth about the war in the Gulf, general."

Powell tried to ignore the interruption, but the man persisted, hectoring him about the civilian dead in the wars in Panama and Iraq, conflicts that brought Powell his national fame. Finally, Powell responded with a patronizing tone, but called the dissenter by name.

"Hi, Ron, how are you? Excuse me, let me answer one question if I may."

"But why don't you tell them, why don't you tell them why—"

"The fact of the matter is—I think the American people are reflecting on me the glory that really belongs to those troops," Powell continued, brushing aside the interruption. "What you're seeing is a reflection on me of what those young men and women have done in Panama, in Desert Storm, in a number of other places—"

"A hundred and fifty thousand people, the bombing—" Ron Kovic's voice could be heard only in snippets beneath Powell's amplified voice.

"—so it's very, it's very rewarding to see this change in attitude toward the military. It's not just Colin Powell, rock star. It's all of those wonderful men and women who do such a great job."

Ron Kovic, a veteran of the Vietnam War and author of the autobiography *Born on the Fourth of July*, did not stop talking that afternoon. From his wheelchair, he struggled to be heard. "I want the American people to know what the general hid from the American public during the Gulf War," Kovic said. "They hid the casualties. They hid the horror. They hid the violence. We don't need any more violence in our country. We need leaders who represent cooperation. We need leadership that represents peace. We need leaders who understand the tragedy of using violence in solving our problems."

How many Iraqi people actually died during the Gulf War in 1991? Powell and other American luminaries of the war have been notably uninterested in discussing that question. But scholar Stephen Zunes wrote in his 2002 book *Tinderbox:* "Most estimates put the Iraqi death toll in the Gulf War in the range of 100,000. Due to the increased accuracy of aerial warfare, the proportion of Iraqi civilians killed was much less than it had been in previous air campaigns. . . . The absolute numbers were quite high. Most estimates of the civilian death toll are approximately 15,000."

During the last several months of 2002, journalists reported that the latest manifestation of Colin Powell's "moderate" resolve was his stance on Iraq within the administration of George W. Bush. But the secretary of state's determination to line up allies and U.N. Security Council backing could be understood as part of a solid commitment to make methodical preparations for the coming war. Powell was thinking very pragmatically in a global context. And so, during a lengthy and pivotal dinnertime presentation to Bush on August 5, he made a strong appeal for building coalitions. Later paraphrased by *Washington Post* reporter Bob Woodward, the Powell pitch to the president emphasized the practicalities of waging war against Iraq: "A successful military plan would require access to bases and facilities in the region, overflight rights. They would need allies."

In early September, four weeks after Powell made his case to Bush, the *Wall Street Journal* noted that "access to Qatar's al Udeid Air Base will be essential to an Iraq invasion." Away from the glare of major publicity, big deals were being cut. "Qatari officials have told U.S. officials that they want a guarantee that the U.S. military presence in Qatar would be permanent," the newspaper reported. "They also want the U.S. to assume a greater portion of the $400 million cost of upgrading al Udeid air base for the U.S. Air Force." As for reluctant members of the U.N. Security Council, some bloody quid pro quos were on the horizon. In the *Journal*'s words, Moscow "is expected to seek an understanding with the U.S. that it will have a freer hand in putting down its rebellion in Chechnya and that it will get a portion of the postwar contracts for rebuilding Iraq." A new spree of atrocities by the Russian army in Chechnya was soon to follow.

As for diplomatic issues, Powell's approach was similar to the outlook of Fareed Zakaria, former managing editor of the elite periodical *Foreign Affairs,* who shared Powell's early interest in urging the return of U.N. weapons inspectors to Iraq, a good public-relations step in the quest for a confrontation leading to war. "Even if the inspections do not produce the perfect crisis," Zakaria wrote in a September 2 *Newsweek* column, "Washington will still be better off for having tried because it would be seen to have made every effort to avoid war." Along similar lines, CNN reported Powell "is working to convince the president of the need to build a strong coalition, similar to the one that existed during the 1991 Gulf War, and win the support of the U.N. Security Council through a new resolution."

Deadly hawks come in many styles; some have polished talons.

Setting the stage for a war against Iraq involved making some very civilized noises, just as for a dozen years the benign-sounding term "sanctions" had masked an enormous toll of death and suffering in Iraq. Aside from some exceptional coverage, the U.S. news media generally ignored the sanctions or flippantly—and falsely—attributed their terrible impact merely to the perfidy of Saddam Hussein. It was just another passing journalistic remark in a *New York Times* article from Baghdad when, on November 18, 2002, the newspaper offhandedly referred to "the impoverishment of many of Iraq's twenty-two million people under the penalties that have been the price for refusal to submit to unfettered weapons inspections." Perhaps a probe of the actual situation would be far too troubling for America.

Erlich: **Sanctions**

Basra once had a swinging reputation. Sheiks from around the Arab world came to the Basra Sheraton to enjoy alcohol, women, and other pleasures formally prohibited in their home countries. Today foreigners can get a rather dilapidated room at that same hotel for forty dollars a night. It costs Iraqis ten.

At the end of 2002, the streets of Basra look like the Gulf War ended only recently. Shell-scarred, rubble-strewn Basra has taken the brunt of two wars. From 1980 to 1988, there was heavy fighting between Iran and Iraq. The area suffered serious damage again from U.S. attacks during the Gulf War in

1991. The now infamous "highway of death," where U.S. planes relentlessly bombed and strafed Iraqi troops who had withdrawn from Kuwait on the last day of the Gulf War, stretched sixty miles from Mutlaa, Kuwait to the outskirts of Basra.

During the Gulf War, President George H.W. Bush called on Iraqis to rise up against Saddam Hussein. Shia Muslims in Basra made the mistake of taking Bush at his word. At the end of the war, the Shias—who are the majority in Iraq—rebelled against the Iraqi Army.

One Iraqi soldier interviewed, a veteran of both the Iran-Iraq and Gulf Wars, had been stationed in Kuwait and retreated from that country when the U.S. attacked. In Basra he suddenly found himself surrounded by angry Shia militia-men demanding that he turn over his AK-47 or die.

"I fought in two wars," the vet said, "and I've never been more scared. Those people were going to murder us." He gave them his rifle, stripped off his uniform, and went home to central Iraq. The veteran belongs to the Sunni Muslim minority in Iraq. He was convinced the uprising was not just against Saddam Hussein, but was the beginning of a Shia-Sunni conflict.

Behind this anecdote lies one of the central contradictions now facing the United States. At the end of the Gulf War, the United States could have removed Saddam Hussein from power, but feared his immediate ouster would fracture the country. Pro-Iranian Shia Muslims would have taken over southern Iraq. Kurds would have seized power in the north, possibly leading to a Kurdish revolt in Turkey.

The same dangers remain today. In 1991 fundamentalist

Shia cleric Muhammad Bakr al Hakim led thousands of his militiamen into southern Iraq from their sanctuary in Iran. This Bakr Brigade fought Saddam Hussein's troops, but also declared an Islamic republic in Basra. The U.S. has opened up talks with Bakr once again, who was seen as having significant support in southern Iraq.

But back in 1991 the Bush administration decided to leave Hussein in power, weaken his regime with economic sanctions, and then oust him within a short period of time. As we know, it didn't work out that way. Saddam Hussein stayed in power by appealing to Iraqi patriotism and through stark repression. The people closest to him profited handsomely from the smuggling of embargoed goods. Mercedes and BMWs plied the streets, and expensive mansions were built along the banks of the Tigris.

The U.S.-imposed sanctions have been brutally effective in bleeding Iraqi civilians. For five years, the domestic economy was in a state of near collapse. The medical system was ruined due to lack of equipment and medicines. Public water and sewage systems deteriorated to the point where children regularly suffered gastrointestinal diseases. Malnutrition became a serious national problem.

In 1990, Iraq was rated 50th out of 130 nations on the U.N. Human Development Index, which measures a country's overall development. By 2000 Iraq had plunged to 126th out of 174. UNICEF estimates that 500,000 children have died as a direct result of sanctions.

As the result of programs established by international agencies and the Iraqi government, child malnutrition rates have improved. In 1996, 11 percent of children were malnourished. By 2002, it was 4 percent. But one million children—one quarter of the children under five—were still acutely malnourished. "This is unacceptable," said Carel de Rooy, head of UNICEF in Iraq. "More still needs to be done to end the suffering of a generation of children."

While the U.S. always stresses that sanctions are mandated by the United Nations, in fact, sanctions would have been lifted long ago were it not for U.S. and British pressure to keep them in place. Sanctions were promoted by Republican and Democratic administrations alike, who blamed Saddam Hussein for the suffering of ordinary Iraqis.

After 1996 the oil-for-food program improved the economy to some degree. It allowed Iraq to sell oil and use 59 percent of the revenues to purchase humanitarian products for those areas of the country controlled by Hussein. The remaining 41 percent went toward Gulf War reparations, funded U.N. programs in the autonomous Kurdish zone in the north, and paid for U.N. administration of Iraqi matters, including weapons inspections.

The oil-for-food program allowed for the import of some food, medicine, and vital spare parts, but the U.S. still worked hard at disrupting civilian life in hopes that it would generate anger at Hussein.

Children's Hospital, Basra

The Basra Children's and Maternity Hospital is a single story building with wings sprawling out via intersecting corridors. It was once a clean and modern structure. At the end of 2002, sections of the hospital were crumbling from lack of repair. Walls needed painting, and the hospital staff sometimes lacked disinfectants to clean floors.

Dr. Asad Eesa, chief resident of the hospital, explained that the cancer wards are empty because the hospital doesn't have enough chemotherapy drugs. Patients come in, are diagnosed, and sent home until medicine becomes available.

Eman Shather couldn't get medicine for her eight-year-old daughter Khanasa, who had an abdominal tumor. Khanasa sat listlessly on the hospital floor. She was about to receive a blood transfusion to alleviate her symptoms, but she really needed chemotherapy treatment.

Dr. Eesa complained that under sanctions, the hospital receives certain chemotherapy drugs one month, and then different drugs the next. The treatment process is so disrupted that relapses often occur. Once an initial drug regimen is disrupted, even getting the correct drug later doesn't help. As a result, Khanasa "has a poor prognosis," said Dr. Eesa, who believes that sanctions are directly responsible for this child's now certain death.

The reality looks very different from the offices of the high-rise U.N. building on New York's east side. An entire U.N. bureaucracy arose to administer humanitarian aid and sanctions against Iraq. A spokesperson for the Office on Iraq, the U.N. department that oversaw the purchase of goods under the oil-for-food program, conceded that delivery of vital drugs was erratic, but press officer Hasmik Egian placed the blame on Saddam Hussein's government. She said bureaucracy and poor priorities are at the root of the problem.

"The government of Iraq is fully responsible for the timely and adequate contracting of supplies," she said. "The health sector has been grossly overlooked by the government."

Barbara Lubin, director of the Middle East Children's Alliance in Berkeley, conceded that the Iraqi bureaucracy can be maddening in its obstinacy. She knows. She's visited Iraq numerous times since 1990. Lubin says that prior to the imposition of sanctions Saddam's government managed to order medicines promptly and provided one of the better free health systems in the Middle East. She says that without question, the U.S.-backed sanctions were responsible for the problems at Iraqi hospitals, and thus for the many unnecessary deaths of Iraqi children.

The Strange Case of the Enriched Cookies

UNICEF is proud of its program to fight malnutrition in Iraq. UNICEF has learned how to fight malnutrition based on experiences in other countries with far worse conditions. The U.N. agency has developed therapeutic milk and enriched cookies (they use the English term biscuits) that help fight against malnutrition among children. UNICEF brings in the milk and cookies, and figures out an equitable way to distribute them. It is simple—except in Iraq.

On the very outskirts of Saddam City, the impoverished slum that is home to an estimated three million Iraqis, the Al Borouj kindergarten was supposed to serve as an example of UNICEF's success in the war against hunger.

At the school, UNICEF and the Iraqi Ministry of Health jointly sponsor a program to screen children for malnutrition. Volunteer health worker Sameera Al Orfali puts the children on a scale to determine if they are severely underweight. Orfali keeps scrupulous records on each of the children. The worst cases are referred to a hospital. She puts others on a list to receive therapeutic milk and enriched cookies that will never arrive.

The cookies disappeared in 2000, according to Orfali, and the milk stopped arriving in 2001. UNICEF had established 2,800 screening centers in schools and childcare centers throughout Iraq, and knows exactly how many malnourished children are seen. But they can't actually provide the needed supplements.

Some international aid workers, on the condition of anonymity, offered an explanation. The U.N. doesn't actually manufacture the dietary supplements. That's done by food manufacturing companies outside Iraq. The U.N. develops strict specifications to make sure the supplements contain all the essential ingredients. The Iraqi government contracts with the manufacturers and then manages delivery.

Under normal international business practices, the purchaser signs a contract with a manufacturer. The purchaser makes the down payment, takes delivery of some of the product, makes sure it meets specifications, and then pays for more, and so on, until the contract is fulfilled. But under the oil-for-food program, after signing a contract, Iraq pays all the money up front.

According to one international aid worker, the enriched cookies didn't meet U.N. specifications when Iraq received them. The company acknowledged the problem, according to the worker, but argued that its cookies still met the nutritional requirements. The Iraqis insisted on sticking to the U.N. specifications.

"The oil-for-food program allows suppliers to take advantage of Iraq by offering cheap goods," said the aid worker. "If all the money has already been paid for the products, then what leverage does the government have?"

After one year, the supplier in question cancelled the contract. The Iraqi government signed a contract with another supplier, but that was also cancelled after a year. Similarly, the Iraqis claimed that the therapeutic milk supplied by another company was contaminated. The company wanted to do its own tests and the dispute wasn't resolved. Meanwhile no milk, no cookies.

The aid workers don't absolve the Iraqi government of all blame in these disputes.

"But the sanctions make everything worse," said one aide worker.

How Drinking Water Became a Tool of War

During the 1970s and 80s, Iraq contracted with European companies to build sophisticated water systems in urban areas, but the treatment plants depended on essential spare parts and chemicals from abroad. Again, sanctions have made crucial maintenance impossible.

As far back as 1991, the U.S. government was aware of the vulnerability of Iraq's water system and the impact sanctions would have on it. Thomas J. Nagy, an associate professor at George Washington University writing in *The Progressive* magazine, uncovered some revealing documents on the Defense Intelligence Agency (DIA) website.

A DIA document dated January 22, 1991, noted that Iraq's water treatment plants depend on "importing specialized equipment . . . to purify its water supply." Without such parts and certain chemicals, "incidences of disease, including possible epidemics, will become probable unless the population were careful to boil water."[2]

Contacted at DIA offices in Virginia, public affairs spokesperson Lt. Commander Jim Brooks said the documents are descriptive, and don't advocate a particular policy. "The accusation is that we wanted sanctions to cause harm." Brooks said that the DIA had been asked what the results would be, and that's what the DIA wrote. He said, "It was an intelligence report."

"When you're going into war, you're worried about a humanitarian crisis," said Brooks. He then explained that good intelligence warns policy makers of possible problems.

For twelve years, largely at U.S. insistence, Iraq had not been allowed to import key spare parts and chemicals needed

2. "Iraq Water Treatment Vulnerabilities;" http://www.gulflink.osd.mil/declass-docs/dia/19950901/950901_511rept_91.html

for water and sewage treatment plants. A confidential United Nations Development Group document dated September 7, 2002, noted that between 1990 and 2000, the daily per capita share of potable water in Iraq dropped by 60 percent in cities and by 63 percent in rural areas. One-fifth of Iraq's population is "at risk for lack of access to safe water and sanitation," according to the report.

Assuming officials read their own DIA reports, the Bush and Clinton administrations were certainly aware of the impact sanctions would have on Iraq's water supply.

From 1991–1999, the Shatt Al Arab Water Treatment Plant in Basra operated at 20 percent of capacity, according to engineer Mehmood Wahad. The U.S. blocked import of certain key parts and chemicals, claiming they could also be used for military purposes. Chlorine, vital for water purification, can also be used to make chlorine gas, for example. Critics say the U.S. intentionally blocked or delayed importation of vital spare parts that have no military use.

"It's a sadistic way of angering the Iraqi people," said Fabio Alberti, president of Bridges to Baghdad, an Italian nongovernmental organization that helps renovate Iraqi water plants. "I really don't understand what kind of military use can be made of chlorinators or pumps."

The United Nations Development Program (UNDP) confirms the long delays in getting such parts. The UNDP rehabilitated a number of water and sewage treatment plants in Baghdad. But the U.N. sanctions committee delayed deliveries of equipment by an average of six months to one year, according to UNDP Deputy Resident Representative Ruth Arias. As a result, she said in an interview, the Iraqis are unable to repair all their water processing facilities. The lack of spare parts also means that untreated sewage is dumped into rivers upstream from water treatment plants—making production of potable water even more difficult.

With the help of Bridges to Baghdad, engineers at the Shatt Al Arab Water Treatment Plant found spare parts inside Iraq and managed to repair the plant in 1999. At the end of 2002, the facility ran at 70 percent of capacity, according to engineer Wahad. He says, technically, the water is safe to drink, but Basra residents don't like the salty taste, and they still get sick.

Asked if he personally drinks his own product, he sheepishly replies, "No. I drink water from private water suppliers."

Solomon: **The March to War**

On November 14, 2002, a few days before the first members of the new U.N. inspection team arrived in Baghdad, the U.S. secretary of defense did an hour-long live interview on the Infinity Broadcasting network. A caller asked what would happen if the U.N. inspectors did not find any weapons of mass destruction in Iraq. "What it would prove would be that the inspection process had been successfully defeated by the Iraqis," Donald Rumsfeld replied. In effect, he was saying that absence of incriminating evidence would be incriminating. "There's no question but that the Iraqi regime is clever," Rumsfeld added, "they've spent a lot of time hiding things, dispersing things, tunneling underground."

Fast approaching was the U.N. resolution's December 8 deadline for Baghdad to submit, with a detailed inventory, an exhaustive declaration of its weapons programs. Citing "pressure on Iraq to give an honest accounting," the *New York Times* reported on November 16: "The United States has indicated that it will consider proof that Iraq has lied sufficient reason to go to war to disarm the government." By the same token, if Iraq admitted to possessing any weapons of mass destruction, that admission might also be deemed sufficient to justify all-out war on Iraq. To avoid war, the Iraqi government had to prove a negative. President Bush would be the judge.

After a four-year hiatus, inspections resumed in Iraq five weeks before the end of 2002. Viewed in the light of hopes for excluding weapons of mass destruction from Iraq's arsenal, the advent of the new inspections—with extremely sophisticated technology and unprecedented intrusive powers—was auspicious. For those in Washington who hoped to clear the way for a war on Iraq, the new inspection regimen was an impediment to be swept aside. "Attempts to kick-start the inspections were complicated yesterday by what Iraqis, publicly, and U.N. officials, privately, say are attempts by the Bush administration to undermine the mission on the outset," the London *Independent* reported on November 20. Intense sniping at head inspector Hans Blix caused a spokesman for the U.N. team on the ground in Iraq, Mark Gwozdecky, to comment: "Those who make these attacks don't seem to understand the damage they are doing to the international attempts to stop proliferation, not just in Iraq, but elsewhere."

But tarring the Blix-led inspection mission ranked as a high priority for war enthusiasts on the Bush team who were eager to pressure Blix into becoming more confrontational with the Iraqi government and perhaps to lay groundwork for discounting his future reports to the Security Council. Key rightwing media voices were warbling from the same songbook. "We hope that as the days unfold Mr. Blix understands that his own credibility is as much on the line as Saddam Hussein's," the *Wall Street Journal* editorialized on November 22, adding darkly that "Mr. Blix has his own track record in Iraq, and it doesn't inspire confidence that he will go to the mat to disarm the dictator. The question now is whether the seventy-four-year-old Swedish diplomat is going to let Saddam make a fool of him and the U.N. one more time." The *Journal*'s editorial page, often the source of opening salvos that quickly resound in the national media echo chamber, was just getting started. Two editions later, a long top-of-the-page attack appeared under the headline "Hans the Timid." As if to be graphic about Blix's dubious character, the drawing that accompanied the op-ed article showed him wearing a tie with a peace sign on it.

Both the editorial and the op-ed piece touted the superior virtues of another weapons inspector, Rolf Ekeus, and complained that he hadn't been chosen for the current post instead of Blix. The editorial called Ekeus "much more tough-minded," and the op-ed described him as "the highly effective leader of the U.N. Special Commission that inspected Iraq in the 1990s," but neither gave so much as a hint to readers that Ekeus was on record denouncing the U.S. government's role in U.N. inspections inside Iraq. Four months earlier, on July

30, the *Financial Times* published a news story that did not interest the American media: "Rolf Ekeus, head of United Nations weapons inspections in Iraq from 1991–97, has accused the U.S. and other Security Council members of manipulating the U.N. inspections teams for their own political ends."

Such manipulation had always been part of Washington's approach to U.N. inspections in Iraq. Now, with the Pentagon mobilizing for full-throttle attack, U.S. policymakers were anxious to denigrate the new inspection process to the extent that they could not control it. The press was sometimes helpful. On Thanksgiving Day 2002, spinners at the White House must have been very appreciative to see the *Washington Post* front-page story with this lead sentence: "The United Nations launched perhaps its most important weapons inspections ever yesterday with a team that includes a fifty-three-year-old Virginia man with no specialized scientific degree and a leadership role in sadomasochistic sex clubs." Among the one hundred weapons experts already chosen to join the U.N. inspection team's advance group in Iraq, the *Post* had found one ("in New York waiting to be sent to Iraq") with an S&M background. The story got major media play across the United States, doing damage to public perceptions of the U.N. inspection effort even though the S&M devotee in question, a former U.S. Marine and ex-member of the Secret Service, had been included on the U.N. inspection team at the suggestion of the U.S. State Department.

The sadomasochism angle provided a convenient wedge for hammering at the new inspection project. According to a follow-up *Post* article that also led with the newspaper's S&M fixation two days later, better-qualified weapons experts with experience inside Iraq during the 1990s had been "deemed to be too aggressive in their disarmament searches" and were excluded from the U.N.'s current inspection team. Among the objections from "former inspectors" was that "the new U.N. policy of not sharing information with intelligence agencies could further handicap the team's ability to find weapons sites." Left unexplained was how a flow of information from the U.N. inspection team to the CIA could aid the U.N. team, though no doubt it would help the U.S. government to fine-tune the selection of targets in Iraq.

During autumn 2002, with U.S. forces converging on the Persian Gulf region, attacks from the air escalated in the north and south of Iraq. A typical American newscast about exchanges of fire came on November 15 when CNN Headline News referred to "U.N.-mandated no-fly zones." The problem here was that the United Nations never "mandated" any such zones. But that didn't seem to matter in Medialand. "Already, U.S. and British warplanes have moved to a more aggressive posture while enforcing Iraq's no-fly zones, the northern and southern regions from which Iraqi planes are banned," *Time* reported in its December 2 issue. The magazine's use of the passive voice ("are banned") facilitated evasion of the fact that the ongoing bombardment by the Americans and the Brits was authorized only by their own say-so.

The stepped-up assaults from the sky were transparently

part of war preparation, and Iraqi anti-aircraft fire enabled the Pentagon to gain useful combat information as well as domestic propaganda points. There was also the possibility that the downing of a plane could serve as a Tonkin Gulf sort of event. "That's always a serious incident, any time anybody fires on American planes," the White House spokesman Ari Fleischer said on November 19. He called it "a material breach of the United Nations resolutions," though U.S. officials backed off the claim after a swift rebuff from U.N. Secretary General Kofi Annan. Still, dropping bombs on northern and southern Iraq was sure to help Washington's war planners. "Airstrikes on Iraqi air defense targets by American and British bombers are beginning to show a pattern that fits neatly into the war plan devised by the Americans for toppling President Saddam Hussein," the London *Times* reported in mid-November. Meanwhile, a Reuters dispatch from the U.S.S. *Abraham Lincoln* explained that the aggressive flights "have become a dress rehearsal for war and a chance to dent Baghdad's military in the run-up to battle."

While the Pentagon readied a massive attack on Iraq, many American news stories depicted the prospect as salutary. In late November, a four-page *Time* spread on the inspections closed with a comment from an atomic agency spokeswoman about old problems: "There were times when we came to a building and the Iraqis were running out the back door. That should not happen now." To which the magazine added an editorial coda: "The best news for the inspectors may be that this time the U.S. is prepared to punish Saddam if it does." In typical fashion, this sum-up of the anticipated war—a way to "punish Saddam"—disregarded and made invisible the people in the line of fire.

Gushing over the military power of Uncle Sam, a *USA Today* feature adhered to the common media pretense that one man would be the target of all that dazzling might: "The B-2 news briefing at Whiteman [Air Force Base] is the latest effort by the Pentagon to advertise the lethal firepower that it will deploy against Saddam in case of war." The newspaper's language was as facile as it was worshipful: "By almost any measure, the B-2 is a technological marvel. It can drop sixteen of the one-ton satellite-guided bombs in a single mission. The bombers, which cost $1.5 billion each, can also carry eight 5,000-pound 'bunker buster' bombs designed to penetrate hardened, underground shelters." The article mentioned in passing that the 5,000-pound warhead was "known in Air Force lingo as 'the crowd pleaser.'" Vast quantities of ink, newsprint, and glossy paper skipped past the actual killing power of this arsenal; so did the many hours of airtime on national television already devoted to war-gaming, complete with full-color simulation graphics and majestic footage of aircraft carriers, jet fighters, sleek bombers, and airborne missiles. Such advance coverage, with its implicit idolatry of American weaponry, was a prefiguration of what could be expected from major U.S. news outlets after the conflagration began.

Making the next war acceptable required the usual blurring of the previous one. (Orwell: "Who controls the past controls the future; who controls the present controls the past.") The lens for perceiving the next war against Iraq had been ground by the successful spin during the Gulf War. "The relentless appetite of broadcasting networks made Pentagon control a simple matter," Patrick J. Sloyan recalled more than ten years after he won a Pulitzer Prize for his coverage of the Gulf War as a *Newsday* correspondent. "Virtually every U.S. weapon system is monitored by television cameras either on board warplanes and helicopters or hand-held by military cameramen or individual soldiers. This 'gun camera' footage may be released or withheld depending on the decisions of political bosses of the military. So when the air war began in January 1991, the media was fed carefully selected footage by Schwarzkopf in Saudi Arabia and Powell in Washington, DC. Most of it was downright misleading."

It was symbolic that the men who had been the Defense Secretary and the Chairman of the Joint Chiefs a dozen years earlier would also be central to the new war, now as vice president and secretary of state. In an essay written when he was a fellow at the Alicia Patterson Foundation in 2002, Sloyan's description of "limitations imposed on reporters on the battlefield" in 1991 had a foreshadowing sound: "Under rules developed by Cheney and Powell, journalists were not allowed to move without military escorts. All interviews had to be monitored by military public affairs escorts. Every line of copy, every still photograph, every strip of film had to be approved—censored—before being filed. And these rules were ruthlessly enforced." As December 2002 began, *Los Angeles Times* media critic David Shaw shared his anticipation with readers: "Based on past performance, both by the current Bush administration and by its immediate Republican predecessors, there's every reason to think that if we go to war against Iraq, Washington will exert more control over the media than ever before, using every tactic from manipulation to deception to disinformation."

Retrospective media critiques have tended to focus on false claims about technical performances: How many "smart bombs" were there really? Didn't most of the Tomahawk cruise missiles stray off course? Didn't the U.S. actually fail to destroy any of Iraq's SCUD missile launchers? But before long, the White House and Pentagon have answers to such questions—the weapons are now superior, and we'll do an even better job next time. "Technology has made the military more efficient," crowed the December 2, 2002, edition of *Time.* The greatest deception of the Gulf War was—and predictably the greatest deception of war against Iraq in 2003 would be—not technical but psychological. Whatever the tensions between press and state, the U.S. media and Washington officials ultimately function as coproducers of illusion. "In manipulating the first and often most lasting perception of Desert Storm," wrote Sloyan, "the Bush administration produced not a single picture or video of anyone being killed. This sanitized, bloodless presentation by military briefers left the world presuming Desert Storm was a war without death."

Such presumptions would certainly surprise the loved ones of the estimated 100,000 Iraqi people who died in "Desert Storm." (Reduced to round numbers, it's difficult for any victims of war to seem like real human beings. "The death of one man is a tragedy," Stalin reportedly commented at Potsdam in 1945. "The death of millions is a statistic.") But a key question is why, with polls indicating majority support for a war against Iraq, it has been deemed necessary to shield those supporters of war from the most basic realities of war. A plausible reason is that the support might collapse under the weight of more real information, especially if conveyed in both intellectual and emotional terms.

"The avowed U.S. aim of regime change means any new conflict will be much more intense and destructive than the [1991] Gulf War, and will involve more deadly weapons developed in the interim," said a report issued in mid-November 2002 by health professionals with the Medact organization and International Physicians for the Prevention of Nuclear War. "Furthermore," they warned, "the mental and physical health of ordinary Iraqis is far worse than it was in 1991, making them much more vulnerable this time round." The report, examining "the likely impact of a new war on Iraq from a public health perspective," found that "credible estimates of the total possible deaths on all sides during the conflict and the following three months range from 48,000 to over 260,000. Civil war within Iraq could add another 20,000 deaths. Additional later deaths from postwar adverse health effects could reach 200,000. If nuclear weapons were used the death toll could reach 3,900,000. In all scenarios the majority of casualties will be civilians."

Even when such estimates were based on the best medical expertise available, they could not be more than educated guesses. The actual extent of the human disaster might turn out to be smaller or larger. But for millions of people, the risks were enormous. The decision-makers ensconced in Washington were eager to roll the dice.

Erlich: **The Oil Issue**

At large demonstrations against U.S. intervention in Iraq you will see placards with that old stand-by, "No War for Oil." Many people believe that oil has played and continues to play a major role in U.S. military decisions about Iraq. After all, Iraq has proven reserves of 112 billion barrels, the second largest of any country in the world after Saudi Arabia. If the U.S. invades and occupies Iraq, why wouldn't U.S. oil companies get contracts and make profits? A pro-U.S. regime in Baghdad would also give U.S. oil companies much greater control of world oil markets. Therefore oil interests play a significant part in determining U.S. policy.

Indeed, 22 percent of the American people believe that oil is the best explanation as to why the U.S. would use military force against Iraq, according to a December 2002 poll. (*New York Times,* 12/5/02)

But that view is subject to mockery in Washington and much of the major U.S. media.

David Ignatius, editor of the *International Herald Tribune,* wrote, "senior Bush administration officials are so busy worrying about weapons of mass destruction that they have paid little attention to oil politics in Iraq. Indeed U.S. oil companies are said to fear they would be excluded from post-war contracts." (*Washington Post* 10/18/02)

American news reporters, pundits and Internet commentators pooh-pooh the concept that oil could influence U.S. political and military policy. But buried in the business sections of U.S. and European newspapers, a different view occasionally leaks out. Let's take a look at some of the major assumptions.

Oil plays a major role in other countries' political and military decisions about Iraq, but not those of the U.S.

According to numerous major media accounts in the U.S., oil interests help determine the policies of other countries regarding Iraq.

French oil company Total Fina Elf has negotiated rights to develop Iraqi fields with total estimated reserves of over ten billion barrels. France boasted $1.5 billion in trade with Iraq during 2001. These factors are often mentioned as a major reason why France fought so hard to modify U.S.-sponsored Security Council resolutions regarding Iraq.

Iraq owes Russia an estimated $8 billion in foreign debt;

Russia's LukOil had $3.8 billion in agreements to rehabilitate and develop Iraqi oil fields. On December 12, 2002, Iraq announced that it had cancelled the contract, apparently out of displeasure with Russia's cooperation with the U.S.

Perhaps U.S. officials used promises of future oil contracts as a bargaining chip to get Putin to acquiesce to a U.S. invasion. Referring to Russia's oil ties to Iraq, President Bush said on Russian TV, "Of course these interests will be taken into account."

"The Russians clearly have interests in Iraq," former U.S. Ambassador to Moscow James Collins told the *Washington Post*. "The question for us is how will those interests be recognized and protected. If you want Russia to be buying into a [U.S. war in Iraq] . . . you need a formula to protect that." (*Washington Post* 10/13/02)

Oil considerations certainly can determine political decisions by other governments, but according to the mainstream media, Bush administration ties to the oil industry are irrelevant. This is all the more curious when we bear in mind that George W. Bush ran an oil company, Vice President Dick Cheney was the CEO of the oil equipment corporation Halliburton, and National Security Advisor Condoleezza Rice served as a member of Chevron's board of directors.

If U.S. oil companies wanted Iraqi oil, they would just buy it. There's no need to go to war.

Some Bush administration supporters argue that if oil were so important, why wouldn't U.S. oil corporations just buy it from Iraq? In fact, if oil companies really controlled

U.S. policy, they would follow the lead of their European counterparts and demand an end to Iraqi sanctions in order to facilitate trade.

As it turns out, this is exactly what U.S. companies did until the 1980s. U.S. and European companies were upset when Iraq nationalized foreign oil holdings in 1972, but they learned to deal with their frustrations. They bought oil from the nationalized Iraqi oil company without much concern for Saddam Hussein's repression of his own people or his military's use of poison gas against Iranian troops and Iraqi Kurds. Business is business. But after 1991, as part of the U.S. effort to topple Saddam Hussein's government through sanctions, U.S. oil companies were prohibited from investing in or buying Iraqi oil, except as approved under the United Nations oil-for-food program.

This probably frustrated U.S. oil executives, who saw lucrative contracts going to companies based in countries where the government had no political conflict with Iraq. For instance, Dick Cheney, as head of Halliburton, actually called for an end to sanctions against Iraq prior to joining the presidential ticket in 2000.

With war looking imminent, U.S. oil companies can doubtless see vast possibilities beyond making limited profits buying oil from a nationalized company. If a pro-U.S. regime privatizes Iraqi oil, then U.S. companies would stand to make billions of dollars by dividing up the industry. It would also give those corporations control over Iraq's substantial oil production, optimally estimated to be ten million barrels a day once the country recovers from the war.

Today Saudi Arabia supplies only 17 percent of U.S. oil, but it plays a key role in the world oil markets. Because Saudi Arabia sits on an estimated 25 percent of the world's total oil reserves, its decisions to increase or decrease production immediately affect U.S. oil company profits. Saudi Arabia has been a staunch U.S. ally, but recently has come under much criticism following the attacks in New York and Washington D.C. on September 11, 2001. If the U.S. installs a client regime in Baghdad, the U.S. oil companies would potentially have far greater influence on world prices. OPEC—of which Saudi Arabia is a leading member—would have far less.

"If you get a regime change and a friendlier government" in Iraq, oil analyst Philip J. Flynn told the *New York Times,* "the spigots will be opened and it'll be a lot harder for OPEC to control prices." (*New York Times* 11/24/02)

Major oil companies are not interested in just earning a fair profit; they need to control as much of the world markets as possible to maximize profits. This means controlling oil at the wellhead, at the refinery, at the distribution points or at the retail level. It also means squeezing the competition.

Mark Flannery, an oil analyst for Credit Suisse First Boston, told MSNBC how a U.S. occupation of Iraq would benefit U.S. oil corporations.

"[If]it's your tanks that dislodged the regime and you have 50,000 troops in the country . . . then you're going to get the best deals. That's the way it works. The French will have men and a 1950s tank. That's just not going to work." (MSNBC 11/11/02)

• • •

Even if U.S. oil companies hope to benefit from a U.S. invasion, they haven't been promised any special deals.

A *Washington Post* columnist quotes Iraqi opposition groups as saying they will review existing Iraqi oil contracts after the overthrow of Saddam Hussein, but "they cautioned that the U.S. companies won't have any inside track. 'This is 2002, not the 1930s or 40s,' said Salah al-Shaikhly, a senior official of the Iraqi National Accord. 'No Iraqi government would last 24 hours if they allowed something like that.'" (*Washington Post* 10/18/02)

Apparently that's not the view of Ahmed Chalabi, the leader of the Iraqi National Congress, who some in the west want to install as the country's next president. In October 2002 he met with executives of three major U.S. oil corporations "to negotiate the carve-up of Iraq's massive oil reserves post-Saddam," according to the London *Observer* (11/3/02).

The article noted that Russian, French, and Chinese oil companies fear being "squeezed out of a post-Saddam oil industry in Iraq. . . . Chalabi has made clear that he would reward the U.S. for removing Saddam with lucrative oil contracts." The *Observer* article exposed the meetings, in part, because British Petroleum is worried that it may also be squeezed out of those lucrative contracts.

Chalabi told the *Washington Post,* "American companies will have a big shot at Iraqi oil." (*Washington Post* 9/15/02)

Regardless of who ends up owning the oil wells and refineries, U.S. oil equipment companies appear ready to gobble up contracts for rebuilding the oil industry. Sanctions and war have significantly reduced Iraq's oil production. U.S. oil equipment companies Schlumberger and Halliburton are well placed to get the estimated $1.5 billion in contracts to rebuild the oil industry, according to a report by Deutsche Bank. (*New York Times* 10/26/02)

It's all a conspiracy theory

The "no war for oil" argument is sometimes attacked as being simply a conspiracy theory. We don't argue that greedy oil company executives phone the White House every day urging war. We have no inside knowledge of what meetings, if any, oil company executives have with the White House. But if discussions are taking place, they certainly would be kept quiet right now. Vice President Cheney won't obey a G.A.O. subpoena to list the energy company executives with whom he discussed energy policy in 2001, so one might assume that disclosures about the present situation will be guarded even more carefully.

No secret cabal need exist, however. The U.S. government—under Republican and Democratic administrations—clearly promotes control of foreign oil resources as an integral part of U.S. "national interests." Somehow the continued profits of U.S. oil companies have become equated with the needs of ordinary people for electricity and transport.

Americans don't benefit from U.S. corporate control of the world's oil markets. We could have a better quality of life were we to use fewer fossil fuels. We could easily reduce gasoline consumption by mandating higher gas mileage for new cars and encouraging public transport. Many environmentally friendly energy sources have become economically viable (wind power, small hydro-electric projects, geothermal systems). Others, such as solar and biomass, are still expensive but could develop rapidly with government assistance. The tax code has subsidized oil and coal companies for years. It seems at least plausible that the government could subsidize these alternative sources until they become more economically competitive with fossil fuel.

Oil isn't the only reason for war

As this chapter has shown, oil is a strong motivating factor in long-term policy towards Iraq. But it's not the only one.

Geopolitics: President Bush proclaimed U.S. opposition to an "axis of evil," consisting of Iraq, Iran, and North Korea. The rest of the world—and many Americans—scratched their heads at the linking of two historic enemies (secular Iraq and the Islamic Republic of Iran) and a hardline Marxist-Leninist state. But now Bush's seemingly harebrained strategy is becoming clearer. Although the three are hardly allies, the Bush administration clearly benefits from toppling each one.

If the U.S. invades and occupies Iraq, it puts tremendous pressure on all other states in the region. Iran will be confronted with tens of thousands of hostile troops on its border and will be concerned about a possible U.S. invasion. Iraq is a major backer of the Palestinian intifadah. Israeli officials will be emboldened, and will hazard still further attacks on Palestinians who seek self-determination.

Military expansion: Remember the peace dividend? At the end of the Cold War, Americans were going to benefit from the closing of military bases around the world and at home. Had a check been cut for this peace dividend, it would have bounced. With each new passing war, the U.S. opens up new "temporary" military bases that become permanent very quickly. Since the war in Afghanistan, the U.S. has established military bases or landing rights in six new countries in the region. As the U.S. ramped up for its war against Iraq, it opened or planned to open new facilities in Qatar, Jordan, Yemen, and Djibouti. It has upgraded existing facilities or increased troop deployments in Turkey, Saudi Arabia, Kuwait, Oman, and Bahrain.

While massive military bases and aircraft carriers are not particularly suited for fighting small groups of terrorists, they do project U.S. political and economic policies into every corner of the globe. U.S. oil company executives wouldn't be holding talks about carving up Iraq's oil fields unless the U.S. military was holding the carving knife.

Wagging the dog: Lots of folks think that the Bush administration whipped up war fever to take people's minds off domestic problems and to help get Republicans elected. Unquestionably, domestic politics play a role in U.S. policy towards Iraq. That's why Bush's senior political adviser Karl Rove sits in on important international policy discussions. Taking a hard line against Saddam Hussein seemed to play well at the polls in November 2002, in part because major Democratic leaders refused to offer any serious opposition to the war plans. Once oil, geopolitics, and military expansion dictate an aggressive policy towards Iraq, then domestic political benefits are a nice dividend.

What to watch for in the future

As this book was written, the U.S. had not yet invaded Iraq. The Bush administration, and its cheerleaders in the media, have ignored or downplayed the oil issue. It will likely be the same after the U.S. effects "regime change." Watch for these issues, and hold the politicians and media accountable.

1. Which international companies receive contracts to rebuild Iraq's oil industry? What percentage are American, British, and European? What percentage come from countries that didn't support the U.S. invasion?

2. Is the Iraqi oil industry privatized? Who buys it and at what price? From what countries do the new owners come and did their governments support the U.S.-led war?

3. If the oil industry is not privatized, what international companies get contracts to help produce Iraqi oil? Are they service contracts, where a company is paid a fee but the Iraqis keep the profits? Or are they based on "shares of production," where the international companies split the profits? (Hint: Oil companies earn less from service contracts.)

4. What happened to the existing oil contracts held by Russian, French and Chinese oil companies?

Afterword by Sean Penn

An Open Letter to the President of the United States of America, which ran as an advertisement in the *Washington Post* on October 18, 2002

Mr. Bush:

Good morning sir. Like you, I am a father and an American. Like you, I consider myself a patriot. Like you, I was horrified by the events of this past year, concerned for my family and my country. However, I do not believe in a simplistic and inflammatory view of good and evil. I believe this is a big world full of men, women, and children who struggle to eat, to love, to work, to protect their families, their beliefs, and their dreams. My father, like yours, was decorated for service in World War II. He raised me with a deep belief in the

Constitution and the Bill of Rights, as they should apply to all Americans who would sacrifice to maintain them and to all human beings as a matter of principle.

Many of your actions to date and those proposed seem to violate every defining principle of this country over which you preside; intolerance of debate ("with us or against us"), marginalization of your critics, the promoting of fear through unsubstantiated rhetoric, manipulation of a quick comfort media, and the position of your administration's deconstruction of civil liberties all contradict the very core of the patriotism you claim. You lead, it seems, through a blood-lined sense of entitlement. Take a close look at your most vehement media supporters. See the fear in their eyes as their loud voices of support ring out with that historically disastrous undercurrent of rage and panic masked as "straight tough talk." How far have we come from understanding what it is to kill one man, one woman, or one child, much less the "collateral damage" of many hundreds of thousands. Your use of the words "this is a new kind of war" is often accompanied by an odd smile. It concerns me that what you are asking of us is to abandon all previous lessons of history in favor of following you blindly into the future. It worries me because with all your best intentions, an enormous economic surplus has been squandered. Your administration has virtually dismissed the most fundamental environmental concerns and therefore, by implication, one gets the message that, as you seem to be willing to sacrifice the children of the world, would you also be willing to sacrifice ours. I know this cannot be your aim so, I beg you Mr. President, listen to Gershwin, read chapters of

Stegner, of Saroyan, the speeches of Martin Luther King. Remind yourself of America. Remember the Iraqi children, our children, and your own.

There can be no justification for the actions of al Qaeda. Ever. Nor acceptance of the criminal viciousness of the tyrant, Saddam Hussein. Yet, that bombing is answered by bombing, mutilation by mutilation, killing by killing, is a pattern that only a great country like ours can stop. However, principles cannot be recklessly or greedily abandoned in the guise of preserving them.

Avoiding war while accomplishing national security is no simple task. But you will recall that we Americans had a little missile problem down in Cuba once. Mr. Kennedy's restraint (and that of the nuclear submarine captain, Arkhipov) is to be aspired to. Weapons of mass destruction are clearly a threat to the entire world in any hands. But as Americans, we must ask ourselves, since the potential for Mr. Hussein to possess them threatens not only our country, (and in fact, his technology to launch is likely not yet at that high a level of sophistication) therefore, many in his own region would have the greatest cause for concern. Why then, is the United States, as led by your administration, in the small minority of the world nations predisposed toward a preemptive military assault on Iraq?

Simply put, sir, let us re-introduce inspection teams, inhibiting offensive capability. We buy time, maintain our principles here and abroad and demand of ourselves the ingenuity to be the strongest diplomatic muscle on the planet, perhaps in the history of the planet. The answers will come.

You are a man of faith, but your saber is rattling the faith of many Americans in you.

I do understand what a tremendously daunting task it must be to stand in your shoes at this moment. As a father of two young children who will live their lives in the world as it will be affected by critical choices today, I have no choice but to believe that you can ultimately stand as a great president. History has offered you such a destiny. So again, sir, I beg you, help save America before yours is a legacy of shame and horror. Don't destroy our children's future. We will support you. You must support us, your fellow Americans, and, indeed, mankind.

Defend us from fundamentalism abroad but don't turn a blind eye to the fundamentalism of a diminished citizenry through loss of civil liberties, of dangerously heightened presidential autonomy through act of Congress, and of this country's mistaken and pervasive belief that its "manifest destiny" is to police the world. We know that Americans are frightened and angry. However, sacrificing American soldiers or innocent civilians in an unprecedented preemptive attack on a separate sovereign nation, may well prove itself a most temporary medicine. On the other hand, should you mine and have faith in the best of this country to support your leadership in representing a strong, thoughtful, and educated United States, you may well triumph for the long haul. Lead us there, Mr. President, and we will stand with you.

• • •

The following statement was read aloud by Sean Penn at a news conference in Baghdad on Sunday, December 15, 2002:

I am a citizen of the United States of America. I believe in the Constitution of the United States, and the American people. Ours is a government designed to function "of," "by," and "for" the people. I am one of those people, and a privileged one.

I am privileged in particular to raise my children in a country of high standards in health, welfare, and safety. I am also privileged to have lived a life under our Constitution that has allowed me to dream and prosper.

In response to these privileges I feel, both as an American and as a human being, the obligation to accept some level of personal accountability for the policies of my government, both those I support and any that I may not. Simply put, if there is a war or continued sanctions against Iraq, the blood of Americans and Iraqis alike will be on our hands.

My trip here is to personally record the human face of the Iraqi people so that their blood—along with that of American soldiers—would not be invisible on my own hands. I sit with you here today in the hopes that any of us present may contribute in any way to a peaceful resolution to the conflict at hand.

Appendix One
A Scoop They'd Rather Forget: U.N. spying scandal goes from fact to allegation

By Seth Ackerman
Contributing Writer, FAIR (Fairness & Accuracy In Reporting)

Nothing makes a newspaper prouder than a juicy foreign-policy scoop. Except, it seems, when the scoop ends up raising awkward questions about a U.S. administration's drive for war.

Back in 1999, major papers ran front-page investigative stories revealing that the CIA had covertly used U.N. weapons inspectors, known as Unscom, to spy on Iraq for the U.S.'s own intelligence purposes. "United States officials said today that American spies had worked undercover on teams of United Nations arms inspectors," the *New York Times* reported (1/7/99). According to the *Washington Post* (3/2/99), the U.S. "infiltrated agents and espionage equipment for three years into United Nations arms control teams in Iraq to eavesdrop on the Iraqi military without the knowledge of the U.N. agency." Undercover U.S. agents "carried out an ambitious spying operation designed to penetrate Iraq's intelligence apparatus and track the movement of Iraqi leader Saddam Hussein, according to U.S. and U.N. sources," wrote the *Boston Globe* (1/6/99). Each of the three news stories ran on the papers' front pages.

At first, U.S. officials tried to deny them, but as more details emerged, "spokesmen for the CIA, Pentagon, White House, and State Department declined to repeat any categorical denials" (*Washington Post*, 3/2/99). By the spring of 1999, the Unscom spying reported by the papers was accepted as fact by other outlets, and even at times defended: "Experts say it is naive to believe that the United States and other governments would not have used the opportunity presented by the U.N. commission to spy on a country that provoked the Persian Gulf War in 1991 and that has continued to tangle with U.S. and British forces," said a *USA Today* news article (3/3/99).

Reluctant to recall

But now that the Bush administration has placed the inspectors at the center of its rationale for going to war, these same papers have become noticeably reluctant to recall Unscom's past spying. The spy scandal badly damaged the credibility of the inspections process, especially after reports that data collected through Unscom were later used to pick targets in the December 1998 bombing of Iraq: "National security insiders, blessed with their unprecedented intelligence bonanza from Unscom, convinced themselves that bombing Saddam Hussein's internal apparatus would drive the Iraqi leader around the bend," wrote *Washington Post* analyst William Arkin (1/17/99).

Suddenly, facts that their own correspondents confirmed three years ago in interviews with top U.S. officials were being recycled as mere allegations from Saddam Hussein. The Unscom team, explained the *New York Times'* Barbara Crossette in an August 3 [2002] story, was replaced "after Mr. Hussein accused the old commission of being an American spy operation and refused to deal with it." She gave no hint that Saddam's "accusation" was reported as fact by her *Times* colleague Tim Weiner in a front-page story three years earlier.

"As recently as Sunday, Iraqi officials called the inspectors spies and accused them of deliberately prolonging their work," the *Washington Post's* Baghdad correspondent wrote in a story casting doubt on the Iraqi regime's current intentions of cooperating (9/8/02). Readers were not reminded that the *Post's* Barton Gellman exhaustively detailed the facts of the spying in a series of 1999 articles.

"Iraq accused some of the inspectors of being spies, because they remained on their host countries' payrolls while reviewing Iraq's weapons," wrote the *Boston Globe*'s Elizabeth Neuffer (9/14/02), in an oddly garbled rendition of the charges. She could have boasted that her paper's own Colum Lynch (now with the *Washington Post*) was widely credited with first breaking the story of Unscom's spying in a January 6, 1999, front-page exposé. But she chose not to. It's hard to avoid the impression that certain media outlets would rather that Unscom's covert espionage had never been exposed in the first place. The day after Barton Gellman of the *Washington Post* first reported the spying charges, in a story sourced to Kofi Annan's office, his own paper ran a thundering editorial denouncing Annan's "gutless ploy" ("Back-Stabbing at the U.N.," 1/7/99) and telling the U.N. leader that he and his aides should have "raised their concerns in private"—rather than sharing them with a reporter for the *Washington Post*.

The Unscom spying scandal is hardly ancient history. The Iraq debate at the U.N. Security Council in the fall of 2002 centered on U.S. demands that the rules for sending inspectors back to Iraq be replaced—because the existing rules, imposed by the council in 1999 in an atmosphere of diplomatic outrage over the spy scandal, limit U.S. control over inspections (*Times of London*, 9/18/02).

Appendix Two
Detailed Analysis of October 7, 2002 Speech by Bush on Iraq

Thank you for that very gracious and warm Cincinnati welcome. I'm honored to be here tonight. I appreciate you all coming.

Tonight I want to take a few minutes to discuss a grave threat to peace and America's determination to lead the world in confronting that threat.

The threat comes from Iraq. It arises directly from the Iraqi regime's own actions, its history of aggression and its drive toward an arsenal of terror.

Chris Toensing, editor of *Middle East Report:* "This might indicate that Iraq is actively threatening the peace in the region. There is no evidence whatsoever that Iraq is doing so, or has any intention of doing so. Other powers are actively disrupting the peace in the region: Israel is trying to crush Palestinian resistance to occupation with brute force, and the U.S. and Britain have bombed Iraq 46 times in 2002 when their aircraft are 'targeted' by Iraqi air defense systems in the bilaterally enforced no-fly zones. Most of our 'friends' in the region—Turkey, Saudi Arabia, Jordan—have strongly urged us not to go to war, and to tone down the war rhetoric. Aren't they better positioned than we are to judge what threatens their safety?"

Eleven years ago, as a condition for ending the Persian Gulf War, the Iraqi regime was required to destroy its weapons of mass destruction, to cease all development of such weapons and to stop all support for terrorist groups.

Rahul Mahajan, author of *The New Crusade: America's War on Terrorism:* "Resolution 687 also speaks of 'establishing in the Middle East a zone free from weapons of mass destruction'— which also means Israel's 200-plus nuclear weapons as well as Syria's and Egypt's apparent chemical weapons capabilities, and any nuclear capability the U.S. has placed in the region."

The Iraqi regime has violated all of those obligations. It possesses and produces chemical and biological weapons.

As'ad AbuKhalil, author of *Bin Laden, Islam & America's New 'War on Terrorism'* and professor of political science at California State University at Stanislaus: "The president fails to credit Reagan's and his father's administrations—prominent members of which included Rumsfeld and Cheney—for their help in the construction of Saddam's arsenal, especially in the area of germ warfare."

Toensing: "After being presented with evidence that Iraq had used chemical weapons to attack the Kurds in 1987-88, the Reagan administration blocked a Senate resolution imposing sanctions on Iraq, and continued to pursue good relations with the regime."

James Jennings, president of Conscience International, a humanitarian aid organization that has worked in Iraq since 1991: "The evidence that Iraq gassed its own people is also not about a current event, but one that happened fourteen years ago. If that did not constitute a good enough reason for going to war with Iraq in 1988 (which the U.S. did not even contemplate at the time), it certainly is not a good enough reason now."

It is seeking nuclear weapons.

Susan Wright, co-author of *Biological Warfare and Disarmament: New Problems/New Perspectives:* "How does Bush know this? It's as if the inspections have already been conducted and we know the outcome. We're expected to accept the administration's word for this without seeing any evidence. We have no way of judging the accuracy of these claims and the only way to do so is to hold inspections. The only country in the region that is known to possess a nuclear arsenal is Israel." [The admnistration says that it does not know if Israel has nuclear weapons: www.commondreams.org/headlines02/0521-06.htm]

Mahajan: "There's no evidence that Iraq has gotten anywhere with seeking nuclear weapons. The pitiful status of evidence in this regards is shown by claims, in e.g. Blair's dossier, that Iraq is seeking uranium from Africa, year and country unspecified. South Africa is, of course, the only country in the continent that has potentially the capacity for enrichment of uranium to bomb quality, and claims not to have supplied Iraq with uranium. Unenriched uranium does Iraq little good, since enrichment facilities are large, require huge investment, and cannot easily be hidden."

It has given shelter and support to terrorism and practices terror against its own people.

The entire world has witnessed Iraq's eleven-year history of defiance, deception, and bad faith.

We also must never forget the most vivid events of recent history. On September 11, 2001, America felt its vulnerability—even to threats that gather on the other side of the earth. We resolved then, and we are resolved today, to confront every threat, from any source, that could bring sudden terror and suffering to America.

Members of the Congress of both political parties, and members of the United Nations Security Council, agree that Saddam Hussein is a threat to peace and must disarm. We agree that the Iraqi dictator must not be permitted to threaten America and the world with horrible poisons, and diseases, and gases, and atomic weapons.

Toensing: "Only two members of the U.N. Security Council would appear to agree with the idea that Iraq threatens, or will threaten, 'America and the world' with weapons of mass destruction, making the next sentence disingenuous at best."

• • •

Since we all agree on this goal, the issue is: How can we best achieve it?

Many Americans have raised legitimate questions: About the nature of the threat. About the urgency of action—and why be concerned now? About the link between Iraq developing weapons of terror, and the wider war on terror.

These are all issues we have discussed broadly and fully within my administration. And tonight, I want to share those discussions with you.

Toensing: "Bush may have shared the discussion, but he did not share the evidence, saying, like the British dossier and CIA reports, that intelligence has established the threat. But Americans apparently will not be seeing it."

First, some ask why Iraq is different from other countries or regimes that also have terrible weapons. While there are many dangers in the world, the threat from Iraq stands alone—because it gathers the most serious dangers of our age in one place.

Iraq's weapons of mass destruction are controlled by a murderous tyrant, who has already used chemical weapons to kill thousands of people. This same tyrant has tried to dominate the Middle East, has invaded and brutally occupied a small neighbor, has struck other nations without warning, and holds an unrelenting hostility towards the United States.

Stephen Zunes, author of *Tinderbox: U.S. Middle East Policy and the Roots of Terrorism* and associate professor of politics at the University of San Francisco: "The hostility toward the United States is a direct consequence of U.S. hostility toward Iraq. Iraq was quite unhostile to the United States when it was receiving support from the United States during the 1980s. The answer is certainly not to appease Iraq's tyrannical regime, as was done in the past. However, to imply this hostility is unrelated to the U.S.

destruction of much of Iraq's civilian infrastructure and other actions during the Gulf War which went far beyond what was necessary to rid Iraqi forces from Kuwait and the U.S.-led sanctions and its impact upon the civilian population is very misleading."

AbuKhalil: "If Bush wants to punish nations that 'tried to dominate the Middle East, has invaded and brutally occupied a small neighbor, has struck other nations without warning' then he would have to punish Israel for an occupation of Palestinian lands that lasted far longer than the now famous (yet brief) Iraqi occupation of Kuwait. Of course, Iraq did attack Iran and Kuwait, and Israel in the span of 30 years has attacked Egypt, Iraq, Tunisia, Lebanon, Syria, Egypt, Jordan, not to mention Palestine, and not to mention a civilian Libyan airliner that was downed by Israeli forces in 1973."

By its past and present actions, by its technological capabilities, by the merciless nature of its regime, Iraq is unique.

As a former chief weapons inspector for the U.N. has said, "The fundamental problem with Iraq remains the nature of the regime itself: Saddam Hussein is a homicidal dictator who is addicted to weapons of mass destruction."

Some ask how urgent this danger is to America and the world. The danger is already significant, and it only grows worse with time. If we know Saddam Hussein has dangerous weapons today—and we do—does it make any sense for the world to wait to confront him as he grows even stronger and develops even more dangerous weapons?

Zunes: "He was far more dangerous in the 1980s when the U.S. was supporting him. It will take many years, assuming military sanctions continue in effect, before he comes close to the strength he had then. If U.N. inspectors are allowed to return, it would be impossible—even if they don't find 100 percent of everything—to get much stronger than he is today."

In 1995, after several years of deceit by the Iraqi regime, the head of Iraq's military industries defected. It was then that the regime was forced to admit that it had produced more than 30,000 liters of anthrax and other deadly biological agents. The inspectors, however, concluded that Iraq had likely produced two to four times that amount.

Zunes: "If this is really a concern, then why did the United States supply Iraq with the seed stock of anthrax spores back in the 1980s?" [William Blum, "Anthrax for Export: U.S. Companies Sold Iraq the Ingredients for a Witch's Brew," *The Progressive*, April 1998, p. 18]

This is a massive stockpile of biological weapons that has never been accounted for, and is capable of killing millions.

Zunes: "This is like saying that a man is capable of making millions of women pregnant. It's a matter of delivery systems, of which there is no proof that Iraq currently has."

We know that the regime has produced thousands of tons of chemical agents, including mustard gas, sarin nerve gas, and VX nerve gas. Saddam Hussein also has experience in using chemical weapons. He has ordered chemical attacks on Iran, and on more than forty villages in his own country. These actions killed or injured at least 20,000 people, more than six times the number of people who died in the attacks of September 11.

Mahajan: "All of this was done with the full support, approval, and connivance of the U.S. government. U.S.-supplied 'agricultural credits' helped fund the sustained counterinsurgency campaign in northern Iraq; the United States supplied military intelligence to Iraq for use against Iran even when it knew Iraq was using chemical weapons in the war; and the United States ran diplomatic interference for Iraq at the U.N."

Toensing: "The U.S. restored diplomatic relations with Iraq in 1984, while it was in the midst of fighting the first of these wars of aggression, because the U.S. wanted to contain the Islamic Revolution in Iran. The U.S. and Britain tilted toward Iraq throughout the war, and U.S. allies in the region, chief among them Saudi Arabia, bankrolled the Iraqi war effort. The U.S. was still trying to become closer to Iraq when it invaded Kuwait."

Zunes: "He attacked Iranian troops because he knew Iran had no allies that would defend it. And we now know that officials from the U.S. Defense Intelligence Agency assisted Iraq in targeting Iranian forces in the full knowledge that they were using chemical weapons. Saddam used chemical weapons against Kurdish civilians because he knew they couldn't fight back. And the U.S. helped cover up the Halabja massacre and other assaults by falsely claiming the Iranians were responsible. In other words, Saddam is a coward. He will use WMDs when he knows he won't have to suffer the consequences, especially when the world's most powerful country is supporting him."

And surveillance photos reveal that the regime is rebuilding facilities that it has used to produce chemical and biological weapons.

Toensing: "That it 'has used.' The last time Bush made a big deal of this, he claimed that Iraq was again using the facilities in this way, an assertion which the IAEA promptly rebutted as unverifiable. It still is unverifiable."

Every chemical and biological weapon that Iraq has or makes is a direct violation of the truce that ended the Persian Gulf War in 1991.

Mahajan: "There are no credible allegations that Iraq produced chemical or biological agents while inspectors were in the country, until December 1998. The reason we don't know whether they are producing those agents or not since then is that inspectors were withdrawn at the U.S. behest preparatory to the Desert Fox bombing campaign."

Yet Saddam Hussein has chosen to build and keep these weapons, despite international sanctions, U.N. demands, and isolation from the civilized world.

[The U.S. has maintained for years that it would continue the sanctions regardless of Iraq's behavior regarding weapons, see "Autopsy of a Disaster: The U.S. Sanctions Policy on Iraq—Myth: The Sanctions Will be Lifted When Iraq Complies with the U.N. Inspections": www.accuracy.org/iraq]

Zunes: "Again, the U.S. has yet to produce evidence that Iraq is building such weapons. Also, U.N. Security Council Resolution 687 calls for Iraqi disarmament as part of a region-wide disarmament effort which the United States has refused to enforce or even support."

Iraq possesses ballistic missiles with a likely range of hundreds of miles—far enough to strike Saudi Arabia, Israel, Turkey, and other nations—in a region where more than 135,000 American civilians and service members live and work.

Toensing: "This is a neat rhetorical trick. Bush knows that Turkey and Saudi Arabia themselves do not feel under threat from Iraq's WMD, so he doesn't claim that. Rather, it's the threat to U.S.servicemen and oil company employees based in those countries which should concern us. The questions left unasked are why Iraq would attack Americans, knowing the massive response that would incur, and of course why so many American troops 'live and work' in Turkey and Saudi Arabia. They're partly there in forward deployment against Iraq."

Zunes: "According to Unscom, 817 of Iraq's 819 Soviet-build ballistic missiles have been accounted for and destroyed. They may possess up to a couple of dozen home-made versions, but none of these have been tested and it is questionable whether they have any functional launchers."

We've also discovered through intelligence that Iraq has a growing fleet of manned and unmanned aerial vehicles that could be used to disperse chemical and biological weapons across broad areas. We are concerned that Iraq is exploring ways of using UAVs for missions targeting the United States.

Toensing: "Other intelligence experts have disputed that UAVs are a threat, because the agents they released might disperse to basically harmless levels by the time they reached the ground if the UAV was trying to cover such a broad area."

Mahajan: "The claim that these UAVs have ranges that would enable attacking the United States, and that they could reach it undetected, is a startlingly new one, and entirely untenable. No one has ever produced evidence of Iraqi capability or intent to target the United States directly."

And, of course, sophisticated delivery systems are not required for a chemical or biological attack—all that might be required are a small container and one terrorist or Iraqi intelligence operative to deliver it.

Mahajan: "Bioterrorist attacks and delivery of biological agents aren't that easy—the very limited effects of the anthrax attacks showed that. In fact, the loss of life in the anthrax attacks occurred mostly among the postal workers who were not issued antibiotics, and not among the congressional staff who were. As for chemical attacks with 'a small container and one terrorist,' they would be severely limited in effect."

And that is the source of our urgent concern about Saddam Hussein's links to international terrorist groups.

Over the years, Iraq has provided safe haven to terrorists such as Abu Nidal, whose terror organization carried out more than ninety terrorist attacks in twenty countries that killed or injured nearly 900 people, including 12 Americans.

Michael Ratner is president of the Center for Constitutional Rights: "Although U.S.intelligence agencies have not found a relationship between Saddam Hussein and al Qaeda, Bush mentions one, but no evidence is shown. Likewise he tries to frighten Americans by talking about the crimes of Abu Nidal, but Abu Nidal is dead. Again it is an attempt to create fear by association with something from the past, not evidence of a current threat."

Iraq has also provided safe haven to Abu Abbas, who was responsible for seizing the Achille Lauro and killing an American passenger. And we know that Iraq is continuing to finance terror, and gives assistance to groups that use terrorism to undermine Middle East peace.

Toensing: "Yes, but neither of these groups is ideologically anti-American. Their attacks are aimed at Israel and Israeli interests, including the killing of Leon Klinghoffer and other Americans. This is a crucial piece of context."

We know that Iraq and the al Qaeda terrorist network share a common enemy—the United States of America. We know that Iraq and al Qaeda have had high-level contacts that go back a decade. Some al Qaeda leaders who fled Afghanistan went to Iraq.

These include one very senior al Qaeda leader who received medical treatment in Baghdad this year, and who has been associated with planning for chemical and biological attacks. We have learned that Iraq has trained al Qaeda members in bomb making, poisons, and deadly gases.

Jennings: "The claim that al-Qaeda is in Iraq is disingenuous, if not an outright lie. Yes, the U.S. has known for some time that up to 400 al-Qaeda-type Muslim extremists, the Ansar al-Islam, formerly 'Jund al-Islam,' a splinter of the Iranian-backed Islamic Unity Movement of Kurdistan, were operating inside the Kurdish security zone set up under U.S. protection in the North of Iraq. For some reason this was kept quiet and has not been much reported in the mainstream media. Finally last Spring the Kurds themselves attacked and killed most of the terrorists in their territory, sending the rest fleeing for their lives across the border into Iran. Since this area was under U.S. protection, and not under Saddam Hussein's rule, it's pretty hard to claim that al-Qaeda operates in Iraq."

Mahajan: "Al-Qaeda has carried out no chemical or biological attacks. The anthrax attacks in the fall of 2001 were almost certainly from a U.S. government employee. It's hard to know what, if anything, to make of claims that one "senior al Qaeda leader" got medical treatment in Baghdad. Giving medical treatment, even to criminals, is not illegal, and with so little evidence given to us, there's no reason to suppose this isn't another story like the one about a meeting between Mohammed Atta and Iraqi intelligence in Prague (now discredited)."

And we know that after September 11, Saddam Hussein's regime gleefully celebrated the terrorist attacks on America. Iraq could decide on any given day to provide a biological or chemical weapon to a terrorist group or individual terrorists. Alliances with terrorists could allow the Iraqi regime to attack America without leaving any fingerprints.

Mahajan: "Biological or chemical weapons would undoubtedly leave fingerprints, just as the anthrax attacks in the fall did. Even if Iraq couldn't be conclusively shown to be the source of such materials, the U.S. government would assume Iraq was the source. Iraq has been under the gun ever since the Gulf War, and can't possibly assume that it could get away with such an attack. Moreover, Saddam has traditionally seen WMD as his ace in the hole, protecting him from defeat. Paranoid dictators do not give control of something they see as the foundation of their security into the hands of networks, like al-Qaeda, which they can't control."

Some have argued that confronting the threat from Iraq could detract from the war against terror. To the contrary, confronting the threat posed by Iraq is crucial to winning the war on terror.

When I spoke to the Congress more than a year ago, I said that those who harbor terrorists are as guilty as the terrorists themselves. Saddam Hussein is harboring terrorists and the instruments of terror, the instruments of mass death and destruction. And he cannot be trusted. The risk is simply too great that he will use them, or provide them to a terror network.

Terror cells, and outlaw regimes building weapons of mass destruction, are different faces of the same evil. Our security requires that we confront both. And the United States military is capable of confronting both.

Many people have asked how close Saddam Hussein is to developing a nuclear weapon. We don't know exactly, and that is the problem. Before the Gulf War, the best intelligence indicated that Iraq was eight to 10 years away from developing a nuclear weapon; after the war, international inspectors learned that the regime had been much closer. The regime in Iraq would likely have possessed a nuclear weapon no later than 1993.

The inspectors discovered that Iraq had an advanced nuclear weapons development program, had a design for a workable nuclear weapon, and was pursuing several different methods of enriching uranium for a bomb.

Toensing: "Yes, inspectors learned all of this—the inspections worked."

Before being barred from Iraq in 1998, the International Atomic Energy Agency dismantled extensive nuclear weapons-related facilities, including three uranium-enrichment sites.

Robert Jensen, author of *Writing Dissent* and an associate professor at the University of Texas at Austin: "Bush at least acknowledged that we know little about Saddam's nuclear capability, but he lied about why. Bush claimed that Iraq barred the inspectors of the International Atomic Energy Agency in 1998. In fact, the inspectors, along with those from the U.N. Special Commission, were withdrawn by their agencies—not expelled by Iraq—in December 1998 when it became clear the Clinton administration was going to bomb Iraq (as it did) and the safety of the inspectors couldn't be guaranteed. The inspectors also spied for the United States, in violation of their mandate."

That same year, information from a high-ranking Iraqi nuclear engineer who had defected, revealed that despite his public promises, Saddam Hussein had ordered his nuclear program to continue. The evidence indicates that Iraq is reconstituting its nuclear weapons program.

Saddam Hussein has held numerous meetings with Iraqi nuclear scientists, a group he calls his "nuclear mujahedeen"—his nuclear holy warriors.

Satellite photographs reveal that Iraq is rebuilding facilities at sites that have been part of its nuclear program in the past.

Toensing: "As Lincoln Chafee said on NPR, if these satellite photos exist, then surely the public has a right to see them. Surely mere photos would not compromise sources and methods." [In 1990, after Iraq invaded Kuwait, the U.S. government claimed that Iraqi troops were threatening Saudi Arabia; this turned out to be false.]

Iraq has attempted to purchase high-strength aluminum tubes and other equipment needed for gas centrifuges, which are used to enrich uranium for nuclear weapons.

Mahajan: "The aluminum tubes can also be used in conventional artillery, which Iraq is allowed to have. In the past, when Iraq tried to build such centrifuges, they used steel tubes. This is an incredibly weak indicator."

If the Iraqi regime is able to produce, buy, or steal an amount of highly enriched uranium a little larger than a single softball, it could have a nuclear weapon in less than a year.

Toensing: "Both the CIA report and the British dossier say that this is very unlikely as long as Iraq remains under sanctions."

Mahajan: "This means only that it has the technological know-how to create the high-explosive 'lenses' necessary to set off the appropriate nuclear chain reaction. As long as it retains its scientists, this will remain the case."

And if we allow that to happen, a terrible line would be crossed. Saddam Hussein would be in a position to blackmail anyone who opposes his aggression. He would be in a position to dominate the Middle East. He would be in a position to threaten America. And Saddam Hussein would be in a position to pass nuclear technology to terrorists.

Mahajan: "Again, such an act is not at all consonant with the history or the mindset of Saddam Hussein. One organization hosted by the Iraqi government, which is classified as terrorist by the State Department, is the Iranian Mujahedin-I-Khalq, whose activities are directed against the current government of Iran. They have never had access to any nonconventional resources from the Government of Iraq. Saddam Hussein sees the radical Islamist terrorist networks like al-Qaeda as a huge potential threat to his own rule, something that concerns him far more than any unrealistic ideas of revenge against the United States. Anything that could allow al-Qaeda (which, in its turn, is likely more concerned with replacing regimes in the Middle East with new radical Islamist regimes) to blackmail him would be the last thing he would give them."

Some citizens wonder: After eleven years of living with this problem, why do we need to confront it now?

There is a reason. We have experienced the horror of September 11. We have seen that those who hate America are willing to crash airplanes into buildings full of innocent people. Our enemies would be no less willing—in fact they would be eager—to use a biological, or chemical, or a nuclear weapon.

Mahajan: "Invoking September 11 without showing any kind of link between the government of Iraq and those attacks is just transparent manipulation. What he really means is that after September 11 he thinks he can get away with such a policy."

Knowing these realities, America must not ignore the threat gathering against us. Facing clear evidence of peril, we cannot wait for the final proof—the smoking gun—that could come in the form of a mushroom cloud.

As President Kennedy said in October of 1962: "Neither the United States of America nor the world community of nations can tolerate deliberate deception and offensive threats on the part of any nation, large or small. We no longer live in a world," he said, "where only the actual firing of weapons represents a sufficient challenge to a nation's security to constitute maximum peril."

Jacqueline Cabasso, Executive Director of the Western States Legal Foundation: "The hypocrisy in this speech—and in the Bush admnistration's overall national security strategy—is monumental. If having weapons of mass destruction and a history of using them is a criteria, then surely the United States must pose the greatest threat to humanity that has ever existed. While Bush warns that 'we cannot wait for the final proof. . . . the smoking gun that could come in the form of a mushroom cloud,' his September 2002 National Security Strategy states that 'America will act against . . . emerging threats before they are fully formed . . . by acting preemptively.' And his top-secret *Nuclear Posture Review*, leaked to the *New York Times* earlier this year, reveals that 'U.S. nuclear forces will continue to provide assurance . . . in the event of surprising military developments . . . Current examples of immediate contingencies include an Iraqi attack on Israel or its neighbors . . . ' It doesn't take a lot of imagination to predict that if Iraq is attacked by the U.S. it might launch whatever it has at Israel—itself a nuclear power. Further, while the U.S. is massively expanding its biological weapons research capabilities—for example by upgrading its bioresearch facilities at the Livermore and Los Alamos Nuclear weapons labs to aerosolize live anthrax and genetically modify bio-organisms—it is blocking a protocol to the Biological Weapons Convention that would allow international inspectors into U.S. facilities. The Bush admnistration's unilateral, headlong rush to war threatens to unleash unprecedented regional instability and potentially catastrophic loss of life. It's hard to image a more self-destructive course of action."

Understanding the threats of our time, knowing the designs and deceptions of the Iraqi regime, we have every reason to assume the worst, and we have an urgent duty to prevent the worst from occurring.

Some believe we can address this danger by simply resuming the old approach to inspections, and applying diplomatic and economic pressure. Yet this is precisely what the world has tried to do since 1991.

The U.N. inspections program was met with systematic decep-

tion. *The Iraqi regime bugged hotel rooms and offices of inspectors to find where they were going next. They forged documents, destroyed evidence, and developed mobile weapons facilities to keep a step ahead of inspectors.*

Eight so-called presidential palaces were declared off-limits to unfettered inspections. These sites actually encompass 12 square miles, with hundreds of structures, both above and below the ground, where sensitive materials could be hidden.

[In fact, there were inspections of these "presidential palaces."]

Zunes: "These are not off-limits. They are open to unfettered inspections as long as an Iraqi official is accompanying the inspectors. Such a proviso is quite legal under U.N. Security Council resolutions authorizing the creation of Unmovic, resolutions that were supported by the United States."

The world has also tried economic sanctions and watched Iraq use billions of dollars in illegal oil revenues to fund more weapons purchases, rather than providing for the needs of the Iraqi people.

Toensing: "Yes, and all the while, the U.S. and Britain were undermining the logic of sanctions and inspections by speaking of regime change, giving the regime no incentive to cooperate."

Mahajan: "The government-instituted food ration program in Iraq has been widely praised, characterized as 'second to none' by Tun Myat, current U.N. Humanitarian Coordinator in Iraq. Money that comes in under the oil-for-food program cannot, despite constant allegations, be used for weapons purchases—all proceeds from such sales are deposited to an escrow account, which is controlled by the U.N. Sanctions Committee. The government of Iraq cannot touch any of this money."

The world has tried limited military strikes to destroy Iraq's weapons of mass destruction capabilities . . . only to see them openly rebuilt, while the regime again denies they even exist.

Mahajan: "For 'world' here, read 'United States and its lieutenant, the United Kingdom.' Those military strikes were a blatant violation of international law, done without Security Council authorization."

The world has tried no-fly zones to keep Saddam from terrorizing his own people . . . and in the last year alone, the Iraqi military has fired upon American and British pilots more than 750 times.

Toensing: "Another remarkable rhetorical trick. The no-fly zones did not protect the Kurds from Iraqi incursions in 1995–96, nor have they protected the Shia or the marsh Arabs from ground-based repression throughout the decade. But rather than mention these somewhat significant failures, Bush concentrates on Iraqi air defenses, which have yet to come close to actually hitting a U.S. or U.K. jet. As with the Saudi-Turkish point above, it appears that U.S.–U.K. attempts to protect the peoples of the region are to be counted as failures because the U.S.and U.K. are in danger."

Francis Boyle, professor of international law at the University of Illinois College of Law and author of *The Criminality of Nuclear Deterrence:* "It is the U.S. government that is violating the United Nations Charter . . . by using military force to allegedly 'police' these illegal 'no-fly' zones that have never been authorized by the U.N. Security Council or by the U.S. Congress, in violation of the 1973 War Powers Resolution as well. Iraq is simply exercising its legitimate right of self-defense under U.N. Charter article 51. The Bush administration has deliberately put U.S. pilots in harm's way in order to concoct a pretext for a catastrophic war of aggression against Iraq. The best way for the American people to protect the lives of our military personnel in the Persian Gulf is to bring them all home."

Mahajan: "Again, the no-fly zones don't involve the 'world,' but are a naked projection of American and British power (France, the third partner in the no-fly zones, withdrew in 1996), unsanctioned by the Security Council."

After eleven years during which we have tried containment, sanctions, inspections, even selected military action, the end result is that Saddam Hussein still has chemical and biological weapons, and is increasing his capabilities to make more. And he is moving ever closer to developing a nuclear weapon.

Clearly, to actually work, any new inspections, sanctions, or enforcement mechanisms will have to be very different. America wants the U.N. to be an effective organization that helps to keep the peace. That is why we are urging the Security Council to adopt a new resolution setting out tough, immediate requirements.

AbuKhalil: "Bush also fails to mention American violations of the sanctions regime, by using the inspectors to spy on Iraq, and to obtain information unrelated to the U.N. mandate."

Among those requirements, the Iraqi regime must reveal and destroy, under U.N. supervision, all existing weapons of mass destruction. To ensure that we learn the truth, the regime must allow witnesses to its illegal activities to be interviewed outside of the country.

And these witnesses must be free to bring their families with them, so they are all beyond the reach of Saddam Hussein's terror and murder.

And inspectors must have access to any site, at any time, without pre-clearance, without delay, without exceptions.

Susan Wright: "[The evidence] suggests that the United States and the United Kingdom intend to set such tough conditions for further arms inspections in Iraq that they would create a double bind. If Iraq rejects the conditions, then war with the United States will follow. If Iraq attempts to comply and an ambiguity triggers action by the security forces of one of the permanent members of the Security Council, which according to this draft, might accompany an inspection team, war could follow anyway. Other members of the Security Council should reject such traps. It is also essential to avoid a situation in which the inspection force is effectively hijacked by the United States and used for espionage, as was the case with the U.N. Special Commission in the 1990s."

The time for denying, deceiving, and delaying has come to an end. Saddam Hussein must disarm himself—or, for the sake of peace, we will lead a coalition to disarm him.

Many nations are joining us in insisting that Saddam Hussein's regime be held accountable. They are committed to defending the international security that protects the lives of both our citizens and theirs.

AbuKhalil: "When Bush speaks about 'many nations' supporting the U.S., he certainly means Israel and U.K., although public opinion in U.K. is running solidly against Bush's war."

And that is why America is challenging all nations to take the resolutions of the U.N. Security Council seriously.

Zunes: "There are well over 90 U.N. Security Council resolutions that are currently being violated by countries other than Iraq. The vast majority of these resolutions are being violated by allies of the United States that receive U.S. military, economic, and diplomatic support. Indeed, the U.S. has effectively blocked the U.N. Security Council from enforcing these resolutions against its allies."

Those resolutions are very clear. In addition to declaring and destroying all of its weapons of mass destruction, Iraq must end its support for terrorism. It must cease the persecution of its civilian population. It must stop all illicit trade outside the oil-for-food program. And it must release or account for all Gulf War personnel, including an American pilot, whose fate is still unknown.

Zunes: "Most of these do not fall under Chapter VII, which allows for the U.N.S.C. to authorize the use of force."

AbuKhalil: "And Bush's sudden concern for U.N. resolutions should not lead one to believe that he will next move to implement all U.N. resolutions—including those against U.S. allies."

By taking these steps, and only by taking these steps, the Iraqi regime has an opportunity to avoid conflict. These steps would also change the nature of the Iraqi regime itself.

America hopes the regime will make that choice.

Unfortunately, at least so far, we have little reason to expect it. This is why two administrations—mine and President Clinton's—have stated that regime change in Iraq is the only certain means of removing a great danger to our nation.

I hope this will not require military action, but it may. And military conflict could be difficult. An Iraqi regime faced with its own demise may attempt cruel and desperate measures. If Saddam Hussein orders such measures, his generals would be well advised to refuse those orders. If they do not refuse, they must understand that all war criminals will be pursued and punished.

If we have to act, we will take every precaution that is possible.

We will plan carefully, we will act with the full power of the United States military, we will act with allies at our side, and we will prevail.

There is no easy or risk-free course of action. Some have argued we should wait—and that is an option. In my view, it is the riskiest of all options—because the longer we wait, the stronger and bolder Saddam Hussein will become. We could wait and hope that Saddam does not give weapons to terrorists, or develop a nuclear weapon to blackmail the world. But I am convinced that is a hope against all evidence.

As Americans, we want peace—we work and sacrifice for peace—and there can be no peace if our security depends on the will and whims of a ruthless and aggressive dictator. I am not willing to stake one American life on trusting Saddam Hussein.

Mahajan: "Throughout all of this, there has never been any credible evidence introduced to indicate that Hussein has any policy of trying to target Americans. His depredations have almost always been distinguished by actions against people that the Western powers don't care about."

Failure to act would embolden other tyrants; allow terrorists access to new weapons and new resources; and make blackmail a permanent feature of world events.

The United Nations would betray the purpose of its founding, and prove irrelevant to the problems of our time. And through its inaction, the United States would resign itself to a future of fear.

That is not the America I know. That is not the America I serve. We refuse to live in fear. This nation—in world war and in Cold War—has never permitted the brutal and lawless to set history's course.

Zunes: "Then why did the United States support Indonesian dictator Suharto for over three decades, as he oversaw the massacre of over a half million of his own people, invaded the tiny nation or East Timor, resulting in the deaths of an additional 200,000? How about brutal and lawless governments in Turkey, Morocco, and Israel that have invaded neighboring countries at the cost of thousands of civilian lives? How about Pinochet and other Latin American tyrants supported by the U.S.?"

Now, as before, we will secure our nation, protect our freedom, and help others to find freedom of their own. Some worry that a change of leadership in Iraq could create instability and make the situation worse. The situation could hardly get worse, for world security, and for the people of Iraq.

The lives of Iraqi citizens would improve dramatically if Saddam Hussein were no longer in power, just as the lives of Afghanistan's citizens improved after the Taliban.

Toensing: "Given what is known about the return of warlordism and chaos to Afghanistan—not to mention the fiction that Afghan women have all thrown away their burqas—this is a debatable proposition, and indicative of the administration's lack of interest in rebuilding Afghanistan. Why would Iraq be any different?"

Mahajan: "On every test of justice and of pragmatism, the war on Afghanistan fails. Worse, every one of these aspects, from an increased threat of terrorism to large numbers of civilian deaths to installation of a U.S.-controlled puppet regime is due to play out again in the war on Iraq. In fact, though it has been little noted, the sanctions regime has made Iraqis dependent on centralized, government-distributed food to survive and relief agencies have already expressed their concerns about the potential for a humanitarian crisis once war starts."

The dictator of Iraq is a student of Stalin, using murder as a tool of terror and control within his own cabinet, and within his own army, and even within his own family.

On Saddam Hussein's orders, opponents have been decapitated, wives and mothers of political opponents have been systematically raped as a method of intimidation, and political prisoners have been forced to watch their own children being tortured.

Jensen: "All of that and more was going on while Iraq was a 'valued ally' of the United States —hence the hypocrisy of the next few sentences."

America believes that all people are entitled to hope and human rights—to the non-negotiable demands of human dignity.

People everywhere prefer freedom to slavery; prosperity to squalor; self-government to the rule of terror and torture.

America is a friend to the people of Iraq.

Anthony Arnove, editor of the book *Iraq Under Siege:* "But the people of Iraq have good reason to feel otherwise. As Nicholas Kristof of the *New York Times* noted in his October 4 report from Baghdad, 'while ordinary Iraqis were very friendly toward me, they were enraged at the U.S. after 11 years of economic sanctions. . . . Worse, U.S. bombing of water treatment plants, difficulties importing purification chemicals like chlorine (which can be used for weapons), and shortages of medicines led to a more than doubling of infant mortality, according to the U.N. Food and Agriculture Organization.' Another war on Iraq—this time, a 'preemptive' attack aimed at 'regime change'—will lead to more civilian casualties and damage to Iraq's infrastructure. And Iraqis are right to worry that the regime Washington installs, in violation of their right to self-determination, will be one that serves U.S. interests, not their own. We should recall the impact of the last war. In the words of Gulf War veteran Anthony Swofford, a former

Marine corporal, writing in the *New York Times*, October 2, 'From the ground, I witnessed the savage results of American air superiority: tanks and troop carriers turned upside down and ripped inside out; rotten, burned, half-buried bodies littering the desert like the detritus of years—not weeks—of combat.' We should be skeptical of Bush's stated concern for the Iraqi people. His real interests in this war are not the Iraq people, or defending Americans from attack, but expanding U.S. hegemony in the Middle East."

Our demands are directed only at the regime that enslaves them and threatens us. When these demands are met, the first and greatest benefit will come to Iraqi men, women, and children. The oppression of Kurds, Assyrians, Turkomans, Shi'a, Sunnis and others will be lifted. The long captivity of Iraq will end, and an era of new hope will begin.

Jennings: "The president has repeatedly claimed, 'We have no quarrel with the Iraqi people.' In his speech to the nation on Oct. 7, he said, 'America is a friend of the people of Iraq.' Try telling that to a friend of mine in Baghdad who walked out of his house following a U.S. bomb attack to find his neighbor's head rolling down the street; or to a taxi driver I met whose four-year-old child shook uncontrollably for three days following Clinton's 1998 'Monicagate' bombing diversion. Try telling it to the mother of Omran ibn Jwair, whom I met in the village of Toq al-Ghazzalat after a U.S. missile killed her 13-year-old son while he was tending sheep in the field. Try telling it to the hundreds of mothers I have seen crying over their dying babies in Iraqi hospitals, and to the hundreds of thousands of parents who have actually lost their infant children due to the cruel U.S. blockade, euphemistically called 'sanctions.' Are the Iraqi people supposed to rejoice now that a new war is being forced upon them by their so-called 'friends?' It is understandable that people are frightened following the disastrous attacks of September 11. But fear is not a good reason to stop thinking. In fact, when we are in danger is when clear thinking is needed most of all."

Iraq is a land rich in culture, resources, and talent. Freed from the weight of oppression, Iraq's people will be able to share in the progress and prosperity of our time. If military action is necessary, the United States and our allies will help the Iraqi people rebuild their economy, and create the institutions of liberty in a unified Iraq at peace with its neighbors.

Later this week the United States Congress will vote on this matter. I have asked Congress to authorize the use of America's military, if it proves necessary, to enforce U.N. Security Council demands.

John Berg, director of graduate studies of the government department at Suffolk University: "Our Constitution makes it clear that Congress, not the President, is to 'declare war'—that is, make the decision that war is necessary in a given situation. For Congress to delegate this determination to the President would be an abdication of its Constitutional responsibility."

Zunes: "According to the articles 41 and 42 of the United Nations charter, this can only be done if the U.N. Security Council finds the violator in material breach of the resolution, determines all non-military means of enforcement have been exhausted, and specifically authorizes the use of force. Otherwise, it will be illegal. Members of Congress would therefore be obliged to vote against it since—according to Article VI of the U.S. Constitution—international treaties such as the U.N. Charter are the supreme law of the land. Furthermore, if the United States can invade Iraq for its violations of U.N. Security Council resolutions, then Britain could invade Morocco, France could invade Turkey, Russia could invade Israel, etc."

Approving this resolution does not mean that military action is imminent or unavoidable. The resolution will tell the United Nations, and all nations, that America speaks with one voice and is determined to make the demands of the civilized world mean something. Congress will also be sending a message to the dictator in Iraq: that his only choice is full compliance—and the time remaining for that choice is limited.

Members of Congress are nearing an historic vote, and I am confident they will fully consider the facts and their duties.

The attacks of September 11 showed our country that vast oceans no longer protect us from danger. Before that tragic date, we had only hints of al Qaeda's plans and designs.

Today in Iraq, we see a threat whose outlines are far more clearly defined—and whose consequences could be far more deadly. Saddam Hussein's actions have put us on notice—and there is no refuge from our responsibilities.

We did not ask for this present challenge, but we accept it. Like other generations of Americans, we will meet the responsibility of defending human liberty against violence and aggression. By our resolve, we will give strength to others. By our courage, we will give hope to others. By our actions, we will secure the peace, and lead the world to a better day.

Phyllis Bennis, author of *Before & After: U.S. Foreign Policy and the September 11 Crisis* and a fellow at the Institute for Policy Studies: "President Bush's speech ignored Congress, and instead was aimed at U.S. public opinion (where his support is dwindling) and international allies in the U.N. (where the U.S. is significantly isolated). It was designed to divert attention from the real reasons for this coming war: oil and empire. It is a war designed to rewrite the political map of the Middle East, and is not dependent on the particular threat posed by a particular dictator. The crimes of the Iraqi regime are serious and longstanding—back to the days of massive U.S. economic and military support, and U.S. provision of the biological seed stock for the anthrax and other germs President Bush warned us about. But launching a massive bombing campaign against Baghdad, a city of more than 5 million inhabitants—grandmothers, kindergarten classes, teenagers—will not secure human rights for those living and dying under those bombs."

[Compiled by the Institute for Public Accuracy on October 8, 2002.]

Appendix Three
An Analysis of the United Nations Security Council Resolution 1441 as Adopted on November 8, 2002

The Security Council, Recalling all its previous relevant resolutions, in particular its resolutions 661 (1990) of 6 August 1990, 678 (1990) of 29 November 1990, 686 (1991) of 2 March 1991, 687 (1991) of 3 April 1991, 688 (1991) of 5 April 1991, 707 (1991) of 15 August 1991, 715 (1991) of 11 October 1991, 986 (1995) of 14 April 1995, and 1284 (1999) of 17 December 1999, and all the relevant statements of its President,

Phyllis Bennis: "According to Secretary of State Colin Powell, 'if Iraq violates this resolution and fails to comply, then the Council has to take into immediate consideration what should be done about that, while the United States and other like-minded nations might take a judgment about what we might do about it if the Council chooses not to act.' In other words, if the Council decision does not match what the Bush administration has unilaterally decided, Washington will implement its own decision regardless. This represents a thoroughly instrumentalized view of the United Nations that its relevance and authority are defined by and limited to its proximity to Washington's positions."

Denis Halliday, a former U.N. Assistant Secretary General who headed the U.N.'s food-for-oil program in Iraq: "Have we really bought the fiction, the Washington propaganda, that Iraq is a threat? We all know—the issue is oil, oil, and more oil. And U.S. control thereof. The new resolution of the U.N. Security Council is a charade, a device to obscure. Nevertheless it is transparent enough that one can point out the trip wires, hoops, and hurdles (combined with dangerous ambiguity) placed so that Iraq must inevitably fail to avoid material breach. Then the Bush war can begin nicely covered in U.N. respectability—although of course it has already begun, what with the 12 years of deadly embargo, the no-fly zone bombings and now placement of army, navy, and air force resources on the ground in the Gulf, Kuwait, etc. Just as in the U.S. military preparations in advance of the 1990 Kuwait invasion, the U.S. is again in training and ready to go—having set up Baghdad yet again. The resolution is little more than a sop to other member states and a response to the domestic pressures that took Bush to the General Assembly in September when he outrageously threatened the entire membership. Pressure on Baghdad to comply will not prevent war—only intense pressure on the Bush regime might. To pretend this resolution represents progress, or is hopeful, or a move in the right direction strikes me as naïve and dangerous."

• • •

James Paul, executive director of the Global Policy Forum which monitors global policy-making at the United Nations, is the author of a series of papers including "Iraq: the Struggle for Oil": "This resolution takes a hard-line approach that will almost certainly lead to war. Thirteen members of the Security Council were opposed to this resolution or deeply skeptical, but Washington used intense pressure and eventually bent them to its will. The U.S. used hardball diplomacy of the type deployed to gain the first Gulf War resolution in 1990. The Secretary of State at that time, James Baker, later described in his autobiography how he lined up votes for resolution 678: 'I met personally with all my Security Council counterparts in an intricate process of cajoling, extracting, threatening, and occasionally buying votes. Such are the politics of diplomacy.'" [For other recent quotes from Paul, see: www.accuracy.org/press_releases/PR092402.htm, www.accuracy.org/press_releases/PR100202.htm]

Francis Boyle, professor of international law at the University of Illinois College of Law: "In 1990, France, the Soviet Union and China all sold Iraq out at the Security Council. . . . Russia can be bought by getting admitted to the WTO and being given a free hand on Georgia and Chechnya, as well as having its oil interests guaranteed in Iraq. China wants an end to proposed high-tech U.S. weapons sales to Taiwan. France wants its oil interests in Iraq protected, as well as its sphere of influence in Francophone Africa respected. The serious bargaining has yet to begin. Meanwhile, Kofi Annan plays the role of Pontius Pilate. Remember that under the U.N. Charter, the U.N. Secretary General is not supposed to be an errand boy for the Permanent 5. And yet he is. The bottom line here is that the Bush Jr. administration originally sought and has now failed to obtain the same language from the U.N. Security Council that the Bush Sr. administration obtained in resolution 679 (1990), authorizing U.N. Member States 'to use all necessary means' to expel Iraq from Kuwait. So a unilateral attack by the United States and the United Kingdom against Iraq without further authorization from the Security Council would still remain illegal and therefore constitute aggression. In recognition of this fact, British government officials are already reportedly fearful of prosecution by the International Criminal Court. And the Bush Jr. administration is doing everything humanly possible to sabotage the ICC in order to avoid any prospect of ICC prosecution of high-level U.S. government officials over a war against Iraq. Lawyers call this 'consciousness of guilt.'"

Recalling also its resolution 1382 (2001) of 29 November 2001 and its intention to implement it fully,

Glen Rangwala, lecturer in politics at Cambridge University, U.K.: "The new reference to 1382, the only resolution mentioned in this paragraph and unmentioned in the previous drafts, is puzzling. Its renewal of the oil-for-food program expired in May 2002 and has been supplanted by 1409 (2002), so the implementation clause is not a commitment to continue the oil-for-food program. Resolution 1382 does not commit the Council to lift economic sanctions—either the import or the export prohibition—upon Iraqi compliance with its disarmament obligations: preambular paragraph 2 of 1382 only lists compliance in disarmament as a necessary, not sufficient, condition for the lifting of sanctions. It is possible that Council members have been mis-sold this part of the resolution. According to reports, certain Council members wanted to relink Iraq's effective and verifiable disarmament to the lifting of sanctions. The U.S. and U.K. may present this preambular paragraph as a concession to this argument, but in reality it is no concession at all." [Resolution 687 called for economic sanctions to be lifted when Iraq complied with weapons inspector, but the

U.S. government has repeatedly stated it would not abide by this, see: www.accuracy.org/iraq]

Recognizing the threat Iraq's noncompliance with Council resolutions and proliferation of weapons of mass destruction and long-range missiles poses to international peace and security,

James Jennings: "The preamble alone provides several possible reasons to attack Iraq irrespective of the operative articles in the body of the resolution. It refers to previous war powers resolutions and reiterates the use of 'all necessary means' to achieve Security Council objectives. It assumes that Iraq is already guilty of proliferation of WMD and has developed prohibited classes of long-range missiles, without reference to Unscom's having dealt effectively with these issues in the past. It is illogical to assume the truth of allegations Unmovic was designed to investigate, when the new inspection regime has not yet taken the field."

Rahul Mahajan: "Claims of a threat posed by Iraq to international peace and security are entirely untenable. Director of Central Intelligence George Tenet refuted Bush's claims in a letter to the Senate, where he said clearly the threat of an Iraqi WMD attack was virtually nonexistent, except possibly in the eventuality of a U.S. war for 'regime change.' Nobody claims Iraq has nuclear weapons, nobody has produced any evidence that Iraq is capable of weaponizing biological agents, and it's quite clear that Iraq can have no more than a nominal chemical weapons capability. When Tony Blair produced a dossier purporting to establish the Iraqi threat, the Labor Party produced a counter-dossier and Glen Rangwala produced notes further to the counter-dossier. Blair is nominally of the Labor Party, and the CIA is part of the Executive Branch, so Bush and Blair can't even get their own people to back up this absurd claim. Even if Iraq had any WMD capacity, nobody has explained why it would risk certain, massive retribution if it either attacked directly or gave weapons to any terrorist organization."

Recalling that its resolution 678 (1990) authorized Member States to use all necessary means to uphold and implement its resolution 660 (1990) of 2 August 1990 and all relevant resolutions subsequent to Resolution 660 (1990) and to restore international peace and security in the area,

Rangwala: "This paragraph is a clear attempt to provide post hoc legal justification for the bombing of Iraq since 1991. It suggests that resolution 678 authorized the use of force to implement all resolutions on Iraq from 1990 to the present day. This is clearly untrue: 678 only justifies the use of force to implement resolutions on Iraq passed between 2 August and 29 November 1990. This is a position that has been repeated by Council members ad nauseum since 1991, with no state but the U.K. and U.S. holding anything other than a literal and meaningful construction of 678."

Mahajan: "The invocation of resolution 678 here is another step in the absurd attempt to claim that 678 somehow justified all use of force against Iraq for all time, if it's in aid of enforcing Security Council resolutions. This would include a claim that 678 justified the imposition of the 'no-fly zones,' a novel claim that no previous administration managed to come up with. Although 678 authorized 'all necessary means' to uphold 660 and 'all relevant resolutions subsequent to resolution 660,' the only reasonable interpretation of the language is to mean all subsequent resolutions up to the time that 678 was passed, not all resolutions for all time to come."

Ratner: "It makes no sense, legal or otherwise, to claim that an earlier resolution can authorize the use of force to enforce subsequent resolutions."

Further recalling that its resolution 687 (1991) imposed obligations on Iraq as a necessary step for achievement of its stated objective of restoring international peace and security in the area,

Deploring the fact that Iraq has not provided an accurate, full, final, and complete disclosure, as required by resolution 687 (1991), of all aspects of its programmes to develop weapons of mass destruction and ballistic missiles with a range greater than one hundred and fifty kilometres, and of all holdings of such weapons, their components and production facilities and locations, as well as all other nuclear programmes, including any which it claims are for purposes not related to nuclear-weapons-usable material,

Deploring further that Iraq repeatedly obstructed immediate, unconditional, and unrestricted access to sites designated by the United Nations Special Commission (Unscom) and the International Atomic Energy Agency (IAEA), failed to cooperate fully and unconditionally with Unscom and IAEA weapons inspectors, as required by resolution 687 (1991), and ultimately ceased all cooperation with Unscom and the IAEA in 1998,

Jennings: "The preamble deplores the fact that Iraq ceased all cooperation with Unscom, but does not indicate why this happened, i.e. confirmed cases of intrusive espionage, which surely would be of concern if the Security Council were genuinely interested in establishing a level playing field for Unmovic's operations."

Sam Husseini, communications director of the Institute for Public Accuracy: "Unscom withdrew from Iraq by issuing a trumped-up report which provided a pretext for the U.S. bombing campaign Desert Fox in December 1998. Some may recall this occurred on the eve of President Clinton's scheduled impeachment vote. Uncom was not only used for espionage, but also as an excuse for bombing. It delegitimized itself as an instrument of weapons inspections. For the Security Council to now one-sidedly blame Iraq for not cooperating with Unscom is absurd." [See: www.accuracy.org/articles/twisted-policy.html]

Mahajan: "Although it's true that Iraq has repeatedly restricted access, its degree of compliance is very high—far higher than the compliance of most nations with regard to binding decisions like Security Council resolutions or judgments of the International Court of Justice. Israel, for example, is in violation of numerous Security Council resolutions with no attempt at progress toward compliance [www.fpif.org/commentary/2002/0210unres.html]. The United States vetoes Security Council resolutions directed against it, as it did with a resolution against its invasion of Panama, and it completely ignored a ruling by the International Court of Justice to cease its terrorist operations against Nicaragua and to pay $17 billion in restitution."

Deploring the absence, since December 1998, in Iraq of international monitoring, inspection, and verification, as required by relevant resolutions, of weapons of mass destruction and ballistic missiles, in spite of the Council's repeated demands that Iraq provide immediate, unconditional, and unrestricted access to the United Nations Monitoring, Verification and Inspection Commission (Unmovic), established in resolution 1284 (1999) as the successor organization to Unscom, and the IAEA, and regretting the consequent prolonging of the crisis in the region and the suffering of the Iraqi people,

Husseini: "This is fundamentally false. It implies that the suffering of the Iraqi people is because of Iraq's non-compliance with the weapons inspectors. That is not true. Contrary to what is stipulated in 687, the U.S. government has repeatedly stated that it would continue the economic sanctions even if Iraq were to fully comply with the weapons inspectors. This means the U.S. policy over the last decade gave a disincentive for Iraqi compliance with the weapons inspectors and ensured an indefinite continuation of the devastating economic sanctions with no legitimate cause." [See: "Autopsy of a Disaster: The U.S. Sanctions Policy on Iraq"]

Rangwala: "This is a pure fabrication: the Council has not made 'repeated demands' that Iraq comply with Unmovic, it has only made one such demand, in resolution 1284 (1999). No resolution subsequent to its creation even mentions Unmovic."

Jennings: "The document goes on record as 'regretting the suffering of the Iraqi people.' One would think that the authors of the resolution were declining attendance at an afternoon tea party rather than admitting complicity in draconian sanctions which have caused the unnecessary death of hundreds of thousands of human beings."

Ratner: "To blame the suffering of the Iraqi people on Iraq is to rewrite history and let the U.S. off the hook. The United States has repeatedly refused to modify the embargo despite efforts by Russia and France to step down the embargo as a result of Iraqi compliance with the inspections of its alleged nuclear weapons research."

Deploring also that the Government of Iraq has failed to comply with its commitments pursuant to resolution 687 (1991) with regard to

terrorism, pursuant to resolution 688 (1991) to end repression of its
civilian population and to provide access by international humani-
tarian organizations to all those in need of assistance in Iraq, and
pursuant to resolutions 686 (1991), 687 (1991), and 1284 (1999) to
return or cooperate in accounting for Kuwaiti and third country
nationals wrongfully detained by Iraq, or to return Kuwaiti proper-
ty wrongfully seized by Iraq,

Rangwala: "By incorporating mention of 688 and regarding Iraq 'ending repression of its civilian population' into a resolution setting out the new standard for Iraqi compliance, the U.S. and U.K. may be leaving the way open to claim that Iraq is not in compliance with the new resolution, even if there is full progress on the disarmament agenda. It is worth noting that the Council has not made reference to 688 in its previous resolutions on Iraq's disarmament—for example, 1284, establishing Unmovic, does not mention 688. That there has now been a change of U.S.-U.K. policy in this regard is an immediate cause for concern."

Jennings: "The allegation of involvement in unspecified 'terrorism' is in itself a possible pretext for war in the current tense political and military climate. If the claim has any substance, it should be detailed in full. If not, it should be abandoned. Perhaps the U.S. Department of State should read the CIA's report, which downplayed this charge against Iraq. The claim that Iraq has 'failed to comply . . . in providing access by international humanitarian organizations to all of those in need of assistance in Iraq' is not strictly true. International assistance agencies have had remarkable access to the entire country for years and a high degree of cooperation from Iraqi officialdom. The word 'all' apparently refers to internally displaced persons, and to prisoners. It would be more accurate to say that certain international organizations, such as the Red Cross, have not been granted access to certain groups of persons, such as prisoners, who may need humanitarian assistance. However, it is not clear that this right is granted to international organizations under the U.N. Charter or existing resolutions, or that any entity other than the government of Iraq has the mandate or responsibility to help 'all' those in need of assistance within the country. In fact, the U.N. and other agencies have expressly not been able to help everybody who needs help, even if they wanted to, because of budget restraints and the vast amount of need. Iraq's recent wholesale release of prisoners may have been an attempt to address this issue and remove it as a pretext for war."

Mahajan: "Iraq has made numerous significant moves to return Kuwaiti property, recently concluding an agreement to return part of the Kuwaiti National Archives. There is no evidence that Iraq has not fully complied with obligations to account for Kuwaiti and third country nationals. It's quite likely that at least some of them were charred beyond recognition by U.S. forces in the so-called 'Highway of Death' massacre, and that Iraq would have no way of accounting for them. . . . Most serious is the insertion of a claim that Iraq has not complied with its 687 commitments to end support for international terrorism. Without more specifics, this is just more innuendo of the kind the Bush administration has repeatedly used to try to connect Iraq with the 9/11 attacks even in the absence of any evidence. One of the few concrete claims made is that Iraq was involved in a supposed plot to assassinate ex-President Bush when he visited Kuwait in 1993. This claim has been thoroughly debunked, by Seymour Hersh among others. The evidence for it was so poor that U.S. officials were reduced to claiming that certain electronic components found in a bomb had a unique signature showing they were Iraqi in origin, while experts said the same construction was widely available in mass-produced transistor radios and similar products."

Recalling that in its resolution 687 (1991) the Council declared that a ceasefire would be based on acceptance by Iraq of the provisions of that resolution, including the obligations on Iraq contained therein,

Rangwala: "This is an even more egregious rewriting of history than those cited above: the draft resolution simply misquotes the Security Council's earlier resolution. The ceasefire was not based on Iraq's acceptance of the provisions of resolution 687: it was based on 'official notification by Iraq to the Secretary-General and to the Security Council of its acceptance' of that resolution (resolution 687, para. 33). The difference is highly significant: the U.S.–U.K. draft text implies that the ceasefire would no longer be operative if Iraq is taken by them as no longer accepting its full disarmament obligations, thus leaving open the justification to use force against Iraq without further Council authorization. The ceasefire is thus portrayed as continually conditional upon Iraqi compliance. This is contrary to the position of every other Council member since 1991: this consistent position has been that the ceasefire can only be terminated if there is new Council authorization to use force. Through this paragraph, the U.S.–U.K. are attempting to award themselves the legal right to use force if they alone perceive Iraq as non-compliant; the abandonment of the specific authorization to use force that was in earlier drafts is thus resuscitated in an oblique but legally equivalent form here."

Determined to ensure full and immediate compliance by Iraq without conditions or restrictions with its obligations under resolution 687 (1991) and other relevant resolutions and recalling that the resolutions of the Council constitute the governing standard of Iraqi compliance,

Jennings: "The resolution leaves no room for mistakes or errors of any kind in its implementation. This approach is unrealistic and unlikely to achieve the Council's wishes, unless the desired result is war."

Recalling that the effective operation of Unmovic, as the successor organization to the Special Commission, and the IAEA is essential for the implementation of resolution 687 (1991) and other relevant resolutions,

Noting the letter dated 16 September 2002 from the Minister for Foreign Affairs of Iraq addressed to the Secretary General is a necessary first step toward rectifying Iraq's continued failure to comply with relevant Council resolutions,

Noting further the letter dated 8 October 2002 from the Executive Chairman of Unmovic and the Director General of the IAEA to General Al-Saadi of the Government of Iraq laying out the practical arrangements, as a follow-up to their meeting in Vienna, that are prerequisites for the resumption of inspections in Iraq by Unmovic and the IAEA, and expressing the gravest concern at the continued failure by the Government of Iraq to provide confirmation of the arrangements as laid out in that letter,

Reaffirming the commitment of all Member States to the sovereignty and territorial integrity of Iraq, Kuwait, and the neighbouring States,

Commending the Secretary General and members of the League of Arab States and its Secretary General for their efforts in this regard,

Determined to secure full compliance with its decisions,

Acting under Chapter VII of the Charter of the United Nations,

1. Decides that Iraq has been and remains in material breach of its obligations under relevant resolutions, including resolution 687 (1991), in particular through Iraq's failure to cooperate with United

*Nations inspectors and the IAEA, and to complete the actions
required under paragraphs 8 to 13 of resolution 687 (1991);*

Michael Ratner: "Stating that Iraq 'has been and remains' in
material breach of prior U.N. resolutions including 687, the cease
fire resolution gives the U.S. government what it wants. It can then
argue that because of this 'material breach' the cease fire is no
longer in effect, and that 678, the 1990 use of force resolution,
governs."

Rangwala: "Iraq, through the letter of its Foreign Minister of 16
September 2002, has made an unconditional offer to allow inspectors into Iraq in order to fulfill all their tasks in line with existing
resolutions. Iraq simply does not 'remain' in breach—material or
otherwise—of any obligations relating to cooperation with
weapons inspectors, as it has fully accepted the existing terms for
the re-entry of inspectors. By labeling compliance as violation, the
message from the Council to Iraq is that acting in accordance with
the terms of the Council's resolutions is a purposeless and unpro-
ductive activity."

Mahajan: "Iraq is certainly technically in 'material breach' of the
obligations stated in 687 and other resolutions. Its compliance or
lack thereof cannot be considered in a vacuum, however—the
United States has from the beginning breached both the spirit and
the letter of the resolutions creating the inspection regime and of
international law. These breaches include its original declaration
(affirmed throughout the past decade by officials like Madeleine
Albright, Bill Richardson, and even by Bill Clinton) that it would
not be bound by 687, but would keep the sanctions on until
Saddam was removed from power—the resolution says clearly
that sanctions will be lifted after the weapons inspectors are satis-

fied. Next, the establishment of the 'no-fly zones' violated Iraq's sovereignty, something explicitly guaranteed by every Security Council resolution on Iraq. The infiltration of spies into Unscom, the previous weapons inspection commission (openly admitted now by Rolf Ekeus, its first head), was a further violation of the inspections process—and among the information they collected was anything that could help target Saddam Hussein for assassination, in violation of both international law and domestic executive order. With Richard Butler as head of Unscom, the U.S. used inspections explicitly to provoke crises, and colluded with him to present a rather innocuous report in December 1998 as a justification for armed attack. Ekeus has noted a pattern of bombing attacks on sites visited by Unscom, more evidence that the United States is illegitimately using inspections for its own national purposes. Without a declaration of all these material breaches, it's impossible to put Iraq's comparatively trivial breaches in proper perspective."

2. Decides, while acknowledging paragraph 1 above, to afford Iraq, by this resolution, a final opportunity to comply with its disarmament obligations under relevant resolutions of the Council; and accordingly decides to set up an enhanced inspection regime with the aim of bringing to full and verified completion the disarmament process established by resolution 687 (1991) and subsequent resolutions of the Council;

Rangwala: "This recognizes that the new resolution is creating a different inspections regime from that agreed in 1991. As such, the resolution is explicitly imposing new obligations on Iraq, in addition to those already accepted. Therefore, the U.S. and U.K. can no longer claim that they are trying to ensure Iraq's compliance with resolutions dating back to 1991."

Ratner: "The resolution arguably does limit the right of the U.S. to go to war immediately by 'afford[ing]' Iraq 'a final opportunity' to comply with the disarmament resolutions and sets up an enhanced inspection regime to achieve this. But, and it is a big but, the resolution goes on in numbered paragraph (4) to state that any 'false statement' or 'omission' in Iraqi declarations or failure to comply with the new resolution constitutes a further 'material breach' and will be reported to the Security Council. Thus, even the most minor omission or disagreement with the inspectors is considered a material breach. Once that is the case, the U.S. can argue not only that Iraq has materially breached the new resolution, but that there is no longer any 'final opportunity' for Iraq to cure its alleged past breaches of resolutions. This then opens the way for the U.S. to make the argument referred to above."

3. Decides that, in order to begin to comply with its disarmament obligations, in addition to submitting the required biannual declarations, the Government of Iraq shall provide to Unmovic, the IAEA, and the Council, not later than 30 days from the date of this resolution, a currently accurate, full, and complete declaration of all aspects of its programmes to develop chemical, biological, and nuclear weapons, ballistic missiles, and other delivery systems such as unmanned aerial vehicles and dispersal systems designed for use on aircraft, including any holdings and precise locations of such weapons, components, sub-components, stocks of agents, and related material and equipment, the locations and work of its research, development and production facilities, as well as all other chemical, biological, and nuclear programmes, including any which it claims are for purposes not related to weapon production or material;

Paul: "This list could be interpreted to mean any chemical or biological product that could be used in a modern economy. Can you imagine the U.S. government being able to produce a list of this type of its holdings in 30 days? The next paragraph of the resolution, which says that any omissions constitute 'material breach,' puts Iraq in a ridiculous bind. Also, according to press reports, the U.S. government will be coming forward with its own lists of what weapons Iraq has. It's possible that we could have a very short inspections process, where the 'evidence' against Iraq's statement is not a finding of the inspectors, but a document from the U.S. government—or possibly planted 'evidence' somewhere in Iraq, which the U.S. government will know the precise location of."

Susan Wright: "Will we now see the U.N. inspections being used for 'regime change' through the back door of some claimed failure of the inspections? Since no clear end game was ever defined by 687 and since it is impossible to prove definitively that Iraq does not have any weapons of mass destruction, this is certainly a grim possibility."

Rangwala: "This paragraph, firstly, raises the barrier for Iraqi compliance; and secondly, may make compliance impossible to achieve at all. It raises the barrier by including items in the list of weapons open to disclosure that were not previously regarded as prohibited. Iraq has not been prohibited from developing aerial vehicles or dispersal systems. The draft resolution compels Iraq now to disclose not only these items but also sub-components and 'related material' of these items. It may make compliance impossible because it, if read literally, is asking for Iraq to provide a full 'declaration of all aspects of its programs' in the chemical field, including those activities not relating to weapons issues. . . . Iraq would be compelled to produce within 30 days a full inventory of all the activities of all the chemical facilities throughout the country, including those engaged in relatively trivial and harmless activities. It is difficult to see how any country could possibly compile and guarantee the validity of such a declaration. Any inaccuracies in this declaration would, in accordance with OP4, constitute a 'material breach' by Iraq of this resolution. As such, this paragraph ensures that the resolution cannot be complied with."

Bennis: "This seems to be an effort to ensure Iraq's inability—regardless of intent—to comply with these very stringent terms. This is asking Iraq to essentially do the initial work of the inspection team itself, cataloguing its entire WMD programs as well as programs never included in the earlier demands. The original inspections mandated in resolution 687 did not include, for example, 'delivery systems, such as unmanned aerial vehicles and dispersal systems designed for use on aircraft, including any holdings and precise locations of such weapons' etc. Resolution 687 also included only long-range missiles, with a range over 150 km, not 'all' ballistic missiles. The terms are significantly stricter here."

4. Decides that false statements or omissions in the declarations submitted by Iraq pursuant to this resolution and failure by Iraq at any time to comply with, and cooperate fully in the implementation of, this resolution shall constitute a further material breach of Iraq's obligations and will be reported to the Council for assessment in accordance with paragraphs 11 and 12 below;

Ratner: "This will be used by the United States as an authorization by it, acting alone and without further U.N. approval, to go to war with Iraq. It will not, according to the U.S., require another resolution by the U.N. to go to war. By labeling alleged past violations of the inspection regime as 'material breaches,' by deeming any further omissions or non-cooperation by Iraq with any of the new inspection regime as 'material breaches' and by repeating the warning of 'serious consequences' for past failures, the U.S. will interpret this resolution as a green-light for war. . . . The U.S. has basically put a gun to the U.N. and said if you don't approve, we will do it anyway. That is not approval the U.N. Charter requires; it is coercion."

Bennis: "This sets Iraq up with a 'damned if you do, damned if you don't' situation. If they claim they have no WMD material to declare, Washington will find that evidence of the 'continuing breach' based on the [unproved but functionally unchallenged] U.S. assertion that Iraq does have viable WMD programs. If Iraq actually declares viable WMD programs, it similarly proves the U.S. claim of continuing breach of resolution 687."

Jennings: "Articles 1 and 2 contain language more or less certain to guarantee a new war if anything goes wrong with the Unmovic omission. Language finding Iraq already in 'material breach' and being given 'a final opportunity' to come clean is a rather ominous way of predetermining the outcome, especially when linked with articles 3 and 4 demanding a full and complete accounting and forbidding any misstatement. This opens the possibility that any missing document page or any evasive statement by any official could trigger a war."

John Burroughs, executive director of the Lawyers' Committee on Nuclear Policy: "As interpreted by the United States government, this assumes that any Iraqi non-compliance with the demand for a declaration of its weapons, materials, equipment, etc., or with the requirements of the inspection regime, would amount to a material breach justifying war by the United States.

This is contrary to basic principles of law. In an ordinary contract, if there has been a material breach, the injured party has the option of declaring the contract void. Here the injured party would be the Security Council, not the United States. And under the U.N. Charter, it is the Security Council that is responsible for the maintenance of international peace and security, the Security Council that is charged with determining whether there is a threat to international peace and security, and the Security Council that is charged with deciding whether use of force is necessary and appropriate to respond to such a threat. . . . It is for the Security Council to decide, unambiguously and specifically, that force is required for enforcement of its requirements. In the weeks and months to come, the burden is on those who claim use of force is necessary. It is fundamental that the U.N. Charter gives priority to the peaceful settlement of disputes and the non-use of force. The Security Council has never authorized force based on a potential, non-imminent threat such as that the United States contends is posed by alleged Iraqi development of nuclear weapons. All past authorizations have been in reponse to actual invasion, large-scale violence, or humanitarian emergency (Korea, Kuwait, Somalia, Haiti, Rwanda, and Bosnia)."

5. Decides that Iraq shall provide Unmovic and the IAEA immediate, unimpeded, unconditional, and unrestricted access to any and all, including underground, areas, facilities, buildings, equipment, records, and means of transport which they wish to inspect, as well as immediate, unimpeded, unrestricted, and private access to all officials and other persons whom Unmovic or the IAEA wish to interview in the mode or location of Unmovic's or the IAEA's choice pursuant to any aspect of their mandates; further decides that Unmovic and the IAEA may at their discretion conduct interviews inside or outside of Iraq, may facilitate the travel of those interviewed and family members out-

side of Iraq, and that, at the sole discretion of Unmovic and the IAEA, such interviews may occur without the presence of observers from the Iraqi government; and instructs Unmovic and requests the IAEA to resume inspections no later than 45 days following adoption of this resolution and to update the Council 60 days thereafter;

Rangwala: "This accords to Unmovic and the IAEA the right to transport anyone—seemingly without his or her permission—outside the country. For example, the resolution would allow Unmovic the right to order senior governmental officials, including the Iraqi leader, to leave the country at their discretion. This accords to Unmovic the legal right to abduct individuals with their families, and to take them abroad. It would be wholly implausible to expect cooperation with such an unchecked range of powers. Even if Unmovic does use this power in a responsible way, the resolution would enable the U.S. to encourage senior Iraqi scientists to defect once they have been taken outside the country. To expect open-ended cooperation from the Iraqi government in such a matter is not plausible. The only way to reach a resolution to the conflict, and to reach the verifiable disarmament of Iraq of its non-conventional weapons, is to set reasonable and achievable standards for cooperation. This is impossible to reconcile with provisions for taking Iraqi individuals outside the country."

Bennis: "The effect of moving scientists and their families outside of Iraq would be to have U.N. arms inspectors acting as asylum officers. Certainly many, perhaps most scientists would jump at the opportunity right now to leave Iraq with their families and be granted asylum somewhere else. They are living, after all, in a country not only devastated by twelve years of crippling economic sanctions and the ravages of a repressive political regime, but also facing the likely possibility of imminent war. There are certainly legitimate reasons why many Iraqi scientists would want to live and work somewhere with greater safety and political freedom. There is also, however, the consequent and understandable likelihood of scientists exaggerating the level of Iraq's military or WMD programs as well as their own role in those programs, in the hope of persuading international immigration officials of their importance."

Jennings: "Enforced capture and transport of Iraqi citizens and their families, meaning if necessary without their consent, as in the Afghan War's Guantanamo Bay detention camp, violates both the Geneva Conventions and the Universal Declaration of Human Rights. The U.S. is bound by treaty to uphold these agreements as part of its international obligations."

Majahan: "Depriving Iraq of its scientifically and technically-trained people is what this amounts to—once they have been seized, removed from the country, and debriefed, they will not feel safe in Iraq. Iraq has already suffered massive 'brain drain' since the Gulf War—the four million expatriates are disproportionately educated and technical people. It has had a 'lost decade' in terms of education as well—the sanctions are responsible for the fact that Iraq, unlike any other country in the world, actually experienced a decrease in literacy in the 1990s. Any more and Iraq's ability to redevelop and reconstruct may be impaired for another generation."

6. Endorses the 8 October 2002 letter from the Executive Chairman of Unmovic and the Director General of the IAEA to General Al-Saadi of the Government of Iraq, which is annexed hereto, and decides that the contents of the letter shall be binding upon Iraq;

Bennis: "This letter asserts a set of arrangements allegedly agreed to by Iraq, without confirmation from Iraq that it did indeed accept those arrangements."

7. Decides further that, in view of the prolonged interruption by Iraq of the presence of Unmovic and the IAEA and in order for them to accomplish the tasks set forth in this resolution and all previous relevant resolutions and notwithstanding prior understandings, the Council hereby establishes the following revised or additional authorities, which shall be binding upon Iraq, to facilitate their work in Iraq:

Bennis: "In general, sidelining existing resolutions and agreements made between Iraq and the United Nations undermines the legitimacy, consistency, and coherence of U.N. resolutions."

Jennings: "Article 7 adds several new and important grants of authority to Unmovic, all of which seem perfectly designed not to work. For example, 'immediate, unimpeded, unconditional, and unrestricted access' to any site is unrealistic in an operational sense, given conditions on the ground in Iraq. The same article cancels presidential sites immunity previously granted in SCR 1154 (1998). The issue of the number of U.N. guards is not addressed in the resolution, perhaps deliberately, meaning that a creeping military occupation could be the outcome, with any resistance leading to war. The size of 'exclusion zones' is left undefined, possibly leaving another opening for an outbreak of conflict. The open-ended range and extent of searches of 'subsystems, records, and materials' may further complicate Umovic's relationships with Iraqi officialdom. If Unmovic searches are conducted in a more aggressive manner than Unscom's searches (as the U.S. and Britain insist, and which Iraq claimed were often unreasonable), then trouble is bound to ensue. This sampling of items raises the question of whether this resolution was designed to succeed or to fail."

• *Unmovic and the IAEA shall determine the composition of their inspection teams and ensure that these teams are composed of the most qualified and experienced experts available;*

Mahajan: "The restrictions on Unmovic personnel put in place by Security Council Resolution 1284 were placed because so many Unscom personnel were essentially employed by the intelligence agencies of the English bloc (the U.S., U.K., Canada, Australia, New Zealand) and acting as their agents, illegitimately transmitting all collected data back to those governments. The clear, and obviously fair, remedy was to require participation from a much broader group of countries and to require lack of any overt links to domestic intelligence agencies of any government."

• *All Unmovic and IAEA personnel shall enjoy the privileges and immunities, corresponding to those of experts on mission, provided in the Convention on Privileges and Immunities of the United Nations and the Agreement on the Privileges and Immunities of the IAEA ;*

Bennis: "Sidelining the existing terms of 1154 (which set special arrangements, including diplomatic accompaniment, for inspection of the eight designated 'presidential sites') undermines the legitimacy of U.N. decision-making."

• *Unmovic and the IAEA shall have unrestricted rights of entry into and out of Iraq, the right to free, unrestricted, and immediate movement to and from inspection sites, and the right to inspect any sites and buildings, including immediate, unimpeded, unconditional, and unrestricted access to Presidential Sites equal to that at other sites, notwithstanding the provisions of resolution 1154 (1998);*

Rangwala: "This provision does away with resolution 1154, which endorsed the memorandum of understanding that created special procedures for the inspection of eight defined and delineated Presidential sites. It firstly causes a new and unnecessary arena for conflict between the U.N. and the government of Iraq. Secondly it demonstrates that agreements with the U.N. are without legitimacy, in that one party to the agreement has acquired a habit of nullifying them when it no longer suits its interests. For the U.N. to abandon the standards of legality in its own resolutions would be to cast a grave aspersion on the United Nations and the fabric of international law."

• *Unmovic and the IAEA shall have the right to be provided by Iraq the names of all personnel currently and formerly associated with Iraq's chemical, biological, nuclear, and ballistic missile programmes and the associated research, development, and production facilities;*

• *Security of Unmovic and IAEA facilities shall be ensured by sufficient U.N. security guards;*

Rangwala: "There is no description of the number or composition of these 'guards.' Iraq is being asked to accept a resolution that permits a foreign military presence on its soil, without knowing the nature of that military presence."

• *Unmovic and the IAEA shall have the right to declare, for the purposes of freezing a site to be inspected, exclusion zones, including surrounding areas and transit corridors, in which Iraq will suspend ground and aerial movement so that nothing is changed in or taken out of a site being inspected;*

Mahajan: "Because the U.S. has gotten so much Security Council opposition, an initial draft that was tailored to be a Rambouillet-style demand for effectively unlimited military occupation, which neither Iraq nor any other sovereign nation could accept, has been dramatically watered down. The provision for ground and air 'exclusion zones' was one of the key elements of that approach, and it has been retained. If Unmovic construes this power broadly enough, it will be an intolerable imposition of the kind that Iraq could not accept. Since Hans Blix has been cooperating closely with the United States, even allowing the U.S. to keep him from sending inspectors back to Iraq, it's not clear the Unmovic will be any more independent of U.S. policy considerations than Unscom was."

Rangwala: "With this provision Unmovic could declare large areas of Iraq to be 'exclusion zones' for an indefinite period of time. Limitations on the authority of inspectors need to be worked into the resolution to preserve a sense of the inspectors' legitimate role, with an obligation imposed on the inspectorate to limit the use of this measure to the environs of specific buildings and only for the duration of a specific inspection. Without such a provision, long-term cooperation between the parties is likely to be subject to periodic crises that would threaten to derail the on-going work of the inspectorate."

• *Unmovic and the IAEA shall have the free and unrestricted use and landing of fixed- and rotary-winged aircraft, including manned and unmanned reconnaissance vehicles;*

• *Unmovic and the IAEA shall have the right at their sole discretion ver-*

ifiably to remove, destroy, or render harmless all prohibited weapons, subsystems, components, records, materials, and other related items, and the right to impound or close any facilities or equipment for the production thereof; and

• *Unmovic and the IAEA shall have the right to free import and use of equipment or materials for inspections and to seize and export any equipment, materials, or documents taken during inspections, without search of Uumovic or IAEA personnel or official or personal baggage;*

Bennis: "The clear language, as written, would allow inspectors to seize and 'export' anything they come across in the course of doing inspections—trucks, computers, carpets—whether or not it has anything to do with prohibited materials or prohibited WMD or missile programs."

Mahajan: "One of the problems with Unscom is that it committed espionage, often involving leaving monitoring equipment behind in places that had been inspected. This provision seems like a way to make sure that Unmovic inspectors could also smuggle such equipment into inspected sites."

8. Decides further that Iraq shall not take or threaten hostile acts directed against any representative or personnel of the United Nations or the IAEA or of any Member State taking action to uphold any Council resolution;

Jennings: "Article 8 in effect demands unconditional surrender of Iraq, a demand not pressed on Iraq during the 1991 postwar cease fire negotiations conducted at Safwan by Gen. Schwarzkopf. Iraq must 'not threaten hostile acts.' The presence of armed guards at any site, or merely slowing or stopping vehicles for normal checks, might be taken as such a threat. This language places the entire Unmovic process in Iraq on a hair trigger war alert. It is difficult to see how conflicts can be avoided under these circumstances."

Bennis: "This language is aimed at demanding Iraqi compliance with the U.S.-British air patrols and bombings going on in the so-called 'no-fly' zones. Neither creation or military enforcement of those zones was ever authorized by the United Nations; no U.N. resolution before this one ever even mentioned 'no-fly' zones. This section would serve to legitimize the eleven-year-long illegal U.S.-British imposition of 'no-fly' zones, and the four-year-long illegal bombing raids carried out there. The U.S. claims that those bombing raids, and the imposition of the zones themselves, are to 'enforce' U.N. resolutions—specifically 688, which calls on Iraq to protect the human rights of various communities. But in fact the bombing is without any actual U.N. authorization. So far the Security Council has never called the U.S. and Britain to account for their illegal actions; this language serves to legalize those actions instead. While not specifying what would constitute 'any member state taking action to uphold any Security Council resolution,' it clearly demands that Iraq allow any action—including illegal military actions—that the U.S. or another country claim is designed to enforce a resolution. It also denies the reality that not all Council resolutions may be enforced with military force at all, even if the Council itself makes the decision. Only resolutions specifically passed under the terms of Chapter VII can lead to the use of force. Resolution 688 was not passed under Chapter VII; quite the contrary, it reaffirms 'the commitment of all Member States to the sovereignty, territorial integrity and political independence of Iraq.'"

9. Requests the Secretary General immediately to notify Iraq of this resolution, which is binding on Iraq; demands that Iraq confirm within seven days of that notification its intention to comply fully with this resolution; and demands further that Iraq cooperate immediately, unconditionally, and actively with Unmovic and the IAEA;

Bennis: "Because there is no specified consequence here for a potential Iraqi delay, it is likely the U.S. will interpret this section as authorizing immediate and unilateral military force. No such force would be appropriate, but there is a history of usurpation of such language."

10. Requests all Member States to give full support to Unmovic and the IAEA in the discharge of their mandates, including by providing any information related to prohibited programmes or other aspects of their mandates, including on Iraqi attempts since 1998 to acquire prohibited items, and by recommending sites to be inspected, persons to be interviewed, conditions of such interviews, and data to be collected, the results of which shall be reported to the Council by Unmovic and the IAEA;

Jennings: "Article 10 blandly invites member states to contribute intelligence and suggest locations for inspections. In addition to potentially causing the process to continue endlessly, the provision can be construed as formalizing another open season for spying on Iraq by its enemies, which is exactly how Unscom got in trouble earlier."

Bennis: "This implies that Unmovic must share its actual findings and raw data with 'the Council,' meaning intelligence operatives from Council member states, including those pledged to overthrow the Iraqi regime (such as the U.S.). When Unmovic was created, its director made clear that his view of intelligence sharing was that it could only be 'one way'—meaning member states could provide Unmovic with information to assist their inspection work, but Unmovic would not provide reciprocity to national intelligence agencies. That would, he rightly recognized, repeat the disaster of Unscom's unauthorized sharing of intelligence material with U.S. intelligence agencies. Calling here for Unmovic to report 'the results' of its interviews and data to the Council indicates a clear U.S. intention to gain access to Unmovic and IAEA data."

11. Directs the Executive Chairman of Unmovic and the Director General of the IAEA to report immediately to the Council any interference by Iraq with inspection activities, as well as any failure by Iraq to comply with its disarmament obligations, including its obligations regarding inspections under this resolution;

Jennings: "Article 11 fails to explain what constitutes 'any interference,' leading to the possibility that a misunderstanding could become a reason for going to war."

12. Decides to convene immediately upon receipt of a report in accordance with paragraphs 4 or 11 above, in order to consider the situation and the need for full compliance with all of the relevant Council resolutions in order to secure international peace and security;

Ratner: "It could be argued that this is the second-stage meeting France and Russia desired and that the consequences of a breach are to be decided by the Security Council. But, by this time, such a meeting may not have any efficacy in stopping the U.S. from making unilateral war. Suppose the Council decides it does not think force is appropriate or reaches no decision—deciding, for example, that Iraq has sufficiently complied. The U.S. might still go to war. It will argue that the Council has already decided that Iraq was in material breach of past resolutions and that any infraction of the current resolution was a 'material breach.' This gives the U.S. all the ammunition it claims it needs for the authority to go to war against Iraq under its theory that the ceasefire is no longer in effect and that the 1990 use of force resolution governs."

Jennings: "Article 12 is actually the war empowerment part of the resolution. It does say that the Council will convene. In the absence of 'full compliance,' the wording directly [in the next paragraph] mentions 'serious consequences.' If such a meeting is held, the Security Council will in effect have a gun to its head, since the U.S. administration has already stated that if the U.N. fails to act, the U.S. will act unilaterally."

Bennis: "This clear language should prohibit any country—including the United States—from acting unilaterally in response to any perceived Iraqi obstruction. However, given Bush administration officials' consistent claim that they need 'no further' U.N. resolutions to authorize the use of force 'to enforce' U.N. resolutions, it is highly doubtful that Washington intends to adhere to this language. The inclusion of the reference 'in order to restore international peace and security' is a code for proceeding immediately to using force, whether or not authorized by a new 'consideration of the situation.' It is certain the Bush administration will point to this reference if they choose to go to war without actual Council consent. The fact that they specifically do not call for an actual formal meeting of the Council, and do not call for a new resolution or new decision, but only the informal call 'to convene' implies a lack of seriousness about the right of the Council alone to determine sufficiency of compliance and possible consequences."

13. Recalls, in that context, that the Council has repeatedly warned

Iraq that it will face serious consequences as a result of its continued violations of its obligations;

Bennis: "The problem is how to define the consequences. Washington uses the term to refer explicitly to military force; for this reason, France and Russia have objected to the use of the term in the new Council resolution. In 1998, when the U.N. Security Council passed a resolution endorsing Kofi Annan's negotiated stand-down with Iraq, the resolution called for 'severest consequences.' At that time, every Council ambassador except that of the U.S. said explicitly that use of the term did not constitute an automatic authorization of the use of force for any country or group of countries. It did not, they said, include what the Russian ambassador called 'automaticity.' The U.S. ambassador, Bill Richardson, alone of all the Council, said, 'we think it does' authorize immediate unilateral use of force."

Jennings: "The word 'consequences' used in this paragraph is a code word for war. It is not at all clear that war is warranted over major or minor disputes that may arise over interpretations of Security Council resolutions. This paragraph prejudges the outcome. It would be better for the international community to wait and see if any degree of non-cooperation by Iraq warrants even thinking of going to war. It is eminently possible that such a drastic step, which the U.S. President claims is the last thing he wants to do, would not be desirable or necessary in any case."

Paul: "The multi-speak coming from Washington allows the allied leaders, and especially the P-5 [Permanent 5] governments, to put a good face on the deal they are striking with Washington. They don't want it to appear that war is 'automatic.' But everyone understands that war is very probable if not inevitable and that the new resolution paves the way for Washington. If it is not so, why are there emergency plans already in full gear to evacuate non-Iraqis from Iraq, to set up refugee camps for those displaced by the fighting, to rush in food to the starving Iraqi population, and (most importantly) to seize and administer the Iraqi oil fields under a U.S. military government. Studies about the legal implications of this latter have been made and it appears that the U.S. will be able to pay for its war and occupation out of the seized oil production, according to sympathetic interpretations of relevant international law. Washington ran a 'profit' on the 1991 war, as they extracted more in 'contributions' from Kuwait, Saudi, Japan, Germany, and others than they actually spent (the term 'profit' was used humorously in Washington at the time). Now perhaps they are going to run a 'profit' again! But, obviously, George is not talking about that aspect of things!"

14. Decides to remain seized of the matter.

Bennis: "This is a fundamental point of principle—it means that the issue of Iraqi requirements and Iraqi compliance remains on the Security Council's agenda, and only the Council itself can make decisions as to future interpretation or enforcement."

Ratner: "We must not forget what this resolution does not do. It does not authorize the United States to go to war against Iraq. Despite claims to the contrary by the United States, that can only happen by means of a second resolution. The U.N. Charter requires specific and unambiguous authorization for the use of force; it is for the Security Council and not the United States to decide the consequences of any failure to implement resolutions."

Majahan: "This makes it unequivocally clear that this resolution would not give the United States the right of unilateral military action. In the past, the U.S. has claimed that 688, which calls on states to help in humanitarian efforts to aid 'minority' groups in Iraq (the Shia are actually a majority) and is not a Chapter VII resolution (i.e. cannot authorize use of force), authorized it to create the 'no-fly zones' and carry out its regular bombing attacks in the course of enforcing those zones. Once again, it's likely that the U.S. will claim this resolution does provide authorization for war, and it will be important to point out that it does not."

[Compiled by the Institute for Public Accuracy on November 13, 2002. Research coordinated by Zeynep Toufe and I.P.A. Communications Director Sam Husseini.]

The authors wish to thank the staff of the Institute for Public Accuracy—Hollie Ainbinder, Sam Husseini, Cynthia Skow, and David Zupan—for their invaluable work and assistance.

Norman Solomon is the founder and executive director of the Institute for Public Accuracy, a consortium of policy researchers and analysts. A nationally syndicated columnist since 1992, he has written ten books including *Unreliable Sources* (with Martin A. Lee) and *The Habits of Highly Deceptive Media*, which won the George Orwell Award for Distinguished Contribution to Honesty and Clarity in Public Language. Solomon's op-ed pieces on media and politics have appeared in the *New York Times*, the *Washington Post*, the *Los Angeles Times* and most other major U.S. newspapers. He is an associate of the media watch group FAIR (Fairness & Accuracy In Reporting).

Reese Erlich started his journalism career thirty-five years ago as an investigative reporter with *Ramparts Magazine*. He taught journalism at San Francisco State and California State University, Hayward for ten years. Freelance reporter Erlich has won numerous journalism awards, including the 2002 prize for best depth reporting (broadcast) from the Society of Professional Journalists, Northern California. He traveled to Iraq on assignment for Canadian Broadcasting Corporation Radio, *The World* (Public Radio International), *Common Ground Radio*, the *St. Petersburg Times* and the *Dallas Morning News*. He is producer of the public radio special documentary hosted by Charlayne Hunter-Gault, "Children of War: Fighting, Dying, Surviving."